One for the Road

One for the Road

Edited by *Stuart Maconie* and *Helen Mort*

smith|doorstop

Published 2017 by
smith|doorstop books
The Poetry Business
Bank Street Arts
32-40 Bank Street
Sheffield S1 2DS
www.poetrybusiness.co.uk

ISBN 978-1-910367-62-9

British Library Cataloguing-in-Publication Data.
A catalogue record for this book is available from the British Library.

Typeset by Utter & Ben Dunmore
Printed by CPI Group (UK) Ltd, Croydon, CR0 4YY
Cover design by Utter & Ben Dunmore

smith|doorstop Books is a member of Inpress,
www.inpressbooks.co.uk. Distributed by NBN International,
Airport Business Centre, 10 Thornbury Road Plymouth PL 6 7PP.

The Poetry Business is funded by the Arts Council

Supported by
ARTS COUNCIL
ENGLAND

Contents

Early Doors: Introduction

Helen Mort

In her introduction to *Green Men & White Swans: The Folklore of British Pub Names*, folklorist Jaqueline Simpson adds a note of caution:

'I cannot guarantee that any pub of which I have written in the present tense will still carry the same name, or even will still exist at all, by the time this book is in the shops a few months hence.' (2011: vii)

In the final stages of editing this anthology, I was driving through Newbold in Chesterfield and gaped from my car window at a huge expanse of space where a distinctive pub called The Wheatsheaf had been just weeks before. You'd hardly know it ever occupied the edge of town. Some British pubs stand derelict, their boarded windows like heavy eyelids, their doors like stopped mouths, strange monuments to the recent past. But others vanish, seemingly overnight.

No matter what physical presence it has, the pub is an imaginative space too, a theatre of dreams, a refuge and an escape. Pubs can be troubled, troubling, haunted and occupied, lost and found. But they are always a part of our cultural imagination. Ever since George Orwell wrote about the 'Moon Under Water' in 1946 - his fictitious, ideal public house - the notion of imaginary pubs has been part of literary discourse. It's the imaginative life of pubs which we've tried to capture in this poetry anthology through writing that evokes and subverts the known world of the bar room and the snug, the beer garden and the cellar. Some of the pubs in these pages are real places you could still find, others are inventions, recollections or predictions, pubs in parallel worlds where you might walk in late at night, dazed from rain, and find that the landlord has already got your order.

In the pages that follow, you'll find praise poems, laments for lost pubs, raised glasses, doomed and celebrated encounters, strange characters at the bar, giddy afternoons and sober reflections. We've featured work from a range of UK poets, from Simon Armitage to Kim Moore, Annie Freud to Luke Wright, each poem selected because it celebrates the pub in a way that isn't straightforward, inviting the reader to look again. Along the way, there are pieces of prose to guide you along your literary pub crawl, from Mark Hailwood's brief history of the origins of the pub to Chris Neilan's account of years spent working behind the bar.

I've worked in several pubs too, from country inns to nightclubs and I've often scribbled poems in quiet moments of shifts. As a legacy from my days as a barmaid, I've come to believe that a poem is like a dram of single malt whisky - concentrated, mind-altering, leaving a sweet sting in the mouth. If that's the case, I hope you get pleasantly drunk on the contents of *One For The Road*.

One for the Road
Stuart Maconie

One winter's afternoon at the end of the 1970s, my English teacher Mr John McDermott, a formidable intellect but a genial, clubbable man with a walrus moustache and a schoolboyish pudding basin crop, tossed a slim volume on the desk in front of me. 'Turn to page 28 and tell me what you make of that then. Me and the lads were arguing in the pub about it.'

The book was a battered schoolroom copy of the *Selected Poems* of Thom Gunn and the poem in question was 'During An Absence'. Mr M claimed that there was a line that had caused some debate over the Marstons and Old Holborn with regard to its meaning, viz. 'our Montague and Capulet are air not individuals / and have no faces for their frowns to hold'. With a swell of callow pride (I was only about 15, come on) I said that it seemed pretty obvious to me; Gunn and his lover were simply a long way apart. Feuding families weren't the problem as they were for Romeo and Juliet, just the tyranny of distance.

It now occurs to me that John McDermott (and possibly 'the lads') knew this, and that he was merely, gently, trying to encourage along this youth from a Wigan council estate into some rich new phase of intellectual development and analysis. He was being a really great teacher. But I did not know that then, as I did not know that Thom Gunn's brilliant, stern, sexy poems were not addressed to girls either, as I blithely assumed them to be in my feverish, girl and poetry-mad teenage imagination. All I knew was that, in the absence of girls, talking about poetry in pubs seemed to me a fabulously glamorous and romantic way to spend an evening. I was somewhere between reading about the Inklings and discovering punk rock, and yet to worry that middle aged men talking poetry in saloon bars was somehow provincial and bachelorish and mildewed. No, back then, the Griffin on Wigan Lane where this discussion took place seemed the Algoinquin Round Table to me, except with John McDermott as Robert Benchley and 'Styx' Hilton – the sepulchral history teacher – as an unlikely Dorothy Parker.

Like beer across a formica table in a snug, the images and themes of pub literature spread across the forms. It isn't just Dylan Thomas three sheets to the wind and declaiming loudly in a cravat. Carol Ann Duffy's 'John Barleycorn', a litany of pub names that become as sonorous and mythic as Barleycorn himself, finds an echo in the very best pop song about a pub, the Arctic Monkey's gorgeous, heartbreaking 'Cornerstone' ('I thought I saw you in the Parrot's Beak, playing with the smoke alarm ...'). Neither of these lovely pieces and indeed hardly any in this fine collection of new verse are about getting drunk in that tiresome old Dylan Thomas bohemian way. They are about pubs as places of companionship and mystery, melancholy and mayhem. You don't have to be a barfly or a beer monster to enjoy knowing that they are there, still part of our cultural heritage and our living world and a place of poetic inspiration, like work and church and hospital and school and football grounds. Something to navigate the days by, a lodestar or a landmark, dragging the compass toward the magnetic north of their warmth, be they in Manchester or Mevagissey.

'Alcohol is the maypole of poetry life,' wrote Ruth Padel. 'Poets don't take many solids, for purely (of course) economic reasons. Poets get paid peanuts ... six drinks and a packet of crisps are standard supper.' This is fun, but is it entirely true? Let's not forget that when dear drunken Dylan fell from that New York barstool (thus establishing a rather reductive pub poetry trope) he did so as a rich rock star touring poet. This is something I remember, as I see some of my poet friends, flanked by security with crackling walkie talkies, making their way to the helipad, doing their VAT returns on a state of the art iPhone while knocking up a terse villanelle. (And this of course, is a joke.)

Samuel Hymes, writing about the great pub-loving poet Louis MacNeice, said 'After the war, in the early Fifties, something went wrong. He tried long poems ... but the wit and vigour of 'Autumn Journal' was gone; the poems are dull and garrulous, like the conversation of someone you might meet in a pub.' Shockingly sniffy. But then Hymes was a professor at Princeton, where maybe they do not have cards of Big D peanuts behind the bar or hot Vimto or the bottle of dusty Cointreau that has not been touched since we had the French exchange student over or quizzes or fights or crying girls (or boys) or any of the things that make pubs a kind of poetry of their own.

'It Was That Kind of Place'

The Best Bar in The World

was an old air raid shelter
up a rural winter alley.

Cans of Stella under the stars
coffee in the morning mist
while the swallows swam the cold
upstream and the train
took flocks of commuters
up the line. After the false dawn

of the TV screen, the window is
a tall white drink of light.
The postman wears a halo.
The bus shelter fills with gold,
spills it onto the platform as a wave
of gulls catches the light on a turn.

Leaves hold a brighter green to the silver
of this waking. Salt sparkles on the path
but the ground is too warm for frost, blue
flowers surprising the eye between the feet.

Tell me, would I see this glory if other people
had not worn me down to this, a brown leaf
spinning in the busy wind, a veined dry thing
not registered by passing eyes?

Ellen McAteer

The Night We Stole a Full-Length Mirror

I'd have walked straight past if you hadn't said
Look at the moon and held my head in your hands
and turned it slowly round to face a skip,
its broken skyline of one-legged chair,
ripped out floor, till I saw it moving
– so slow, so bright – across the silver glass.
We stood there for ages, a bit drunk
staring at the moon hanging there
as if it were for sale and we an old couple
weighing it up but knowing in our hearts
it is beyond us – A cat jumps out
and before we know it we're stealing back to my flat,
the great thing like a masterpiece in our hands,
its surface anxious with knees and knuckles,
the clenched line of your jaw and your lips
kissing the glass over and over with curses.
You lean it so it catches the bed and me,
I nudge it with my toe so it won't hold my head.
Switching off the light my skin turns blue
and when you come in on the scene and we see
ourselves like this we start to move like real
professionals and my head, disowned and free,
watches what our bodies are doing and somewhere
the thought *I can't believe we weren't made for this*
and I can't stop looking even though the ache
in my throat is growing and soon there will be tears
and I can hear you looking and I know what you're
looking at and it doesn't matter but it isn't me.
You left me behind in a bar in Copenhagen St,
the one with the small red lamps and my face hung
a hundred identical times along the stained wall
invoking like some old speaking doll
the dissatisfaction I come back and back to
and there's this really pretty Chinese waitress
you're trying not to look at while I'm talking to you.
Then you get up and I'm left alone so I lift my head to look

at the man who's been staring at me since I walked in.
He's huge and lonely and lifts his glass and nods
and all the women along the wall break into smiles.
Then you're back and whispering *your breasts your breasts*
and your hands are scrambling up the wet stone
of my back and I imagine the lonely man is there
behind the silver screen sipping his drink,
his eyes thick and moist behind the glass;
I know he's waiting to catch my eye but I won't
be seen to know I'm being watched. Not
till it's over and we collapse, all of a sudden
and awkward, and the room becomes itself again,
filling the mirror with its things and our two faces
staring in, calm and dull and self-absorbed.
Then we look at each other and are surprised
as if we weren't expecting to find the other
here and the smile is quick, like a nod slipped in
between two conspirators returned to the world
of daylight, birdsong, the good tug of guilt
before we tilt the mirror up-, sky-, heaven-ward.

Greta Stoddart

Immortality for Jewish Girls

I used to think I was good at drink,
pub life and the swinging door,
waving a tenner with a meaningful look,
versatile, opinionated, gregarious,
always with a funny story
and the unexpected
request for Angostura Bitters in my Pinot Grigio.
In these latter days,
as the sky darkens at four
and the wind blows the wet leaves
airborne,
the promise of alcohol
dews my lip
and I look fondly back on
The Rosendale,
The Bedford,
The Samuel Beckett and The Shakespeare,
The Blue Posts,
The Old Ship's double entrance and the Auld Shillelagh's tiny bar,
The Sun where we foregathered and the Blacksmith's Head
where we got married,
The Cock Tavern
The Wheatsheaf
and The Coach and Horses
with its Richard Harris look-a-likes –
I'm still telling the same
old story.

Annie Freud

Iohannes of Sutton

Effeta, [...] Be thou openyd.
And anoon hise eris weren
openyd. (Mark, VII: 34-35)

Sunday disco, Hacienda:
mirrorball, Hazell Dean,
drink-drive XR3 –
searchin, lookin for love.

Gary Davies back-perm DJ –
oooh. Mandy does/Mandy doesn't;
back-room snooker, potting
the brown and the pink.

What? Puking by the bins.
She sucked her finger
and poked it in my ear –
better move on down the line.

Steve Ely

A Surfeit of Jelly Beans

Trophy was the bitter, the big-headed pint
that thinks it's a quart. I was full of it,
bleached hair, painted leather, the ruffs and frills
of a Restoration dandy. I switched
to the beau monde's cocktail of choice, vodka
and Pernod, topped-off with sugary black.
By Auld Lang Syne I was lurching puff-cheeked
for the exit, wrestling revellers aside.
I didn't make it, puking sweet purple
over her shoulder, before falling through the door
to chuck-up my guts on the salt of the frozen car park.
She staggered me home over ice-rut pavements,
over and over repeating her number,
which my wasted heart remembered, and now I forget.

Steve Ely

The Jacket

We read our banns to strangers, in grip
of gormless love. Our idiot rapture
seduced the streets to smiles: we showered
in confetti of bemused congratulation.

Sipping childish cider in shit-hole pubs,
barmaids called us love's young dream
and told us get a room. But heaven and earth
could not contain the fervour of our passion.

Gallant I gave her my envied jacket,
a red leather from X-Clothes in Leeds.
I cloaked it over her flowery shoulders
in a rite of debt and devotion. I would have
given her the world and everything in it —
my love, my honey, my harp. I gave her away.

Steve Ely

Mind Your Head on the Light

In the days when this town was grim, unreconstructed, it stood proud
in the wasteland between the two big streets, Conway and Cleveland,
where, back in the fifties, terraces had collapsed under a blitzkrieg of smart
planners, and towers had been thrown up (Oak and Eldon *Gardens*, those
concrete sequoias perverting nature); which, two decades on and the
dream grown shabby, fell out of fashion – fell through dynamite's passion
– leaving this place alone in a grid of pointless roads, a grade-A slap-up
Victorian boozer.

THE ANGEL INN FREE HOUSE, brown letters on the sheer cream
wall facing the walk from the precinct. No locals, so both dispossessed
and daring (flirting with the rough edge) called it theirs, greasers one end,
casuals the other; Marston's Pedigree pumped while the jukebox thumped
out faded hits – *More Than a Feeling, Hotel California, Sultans of Swing,
Since You Been Gone*. Hey, Paulo: remember that night you danced on the
table? *Mind your head on the light* was all the barman said, it was that kind
of place.

Alan Buckley

The Swan

That night, on lanes too small for the map,
we turned at a sign in the hedge, crossed
the border, saw a swan sat high on a porch
and not knowing what we'd find, opened
a low door to pass out of the dark
and into a room of flickered malty brown
like the glint of a full pint glass.

We sat on a settle next to a fox.
The landlady came through, fussy
and framed among bottles of Butty Bach.
No pumps. No music. Slow clock tick.
Then a man and his two lads driven
from Abergavenny, and—*Evenin' John*—
a bony man and a squeaky woman

who sat on her own but might have been
with him. Later, the landlady stepped out
of her frame to give our Jack something,
then pulled up a chair to tell us how she came
from a town in the South a life ago,
never married and somehow never left.
We were bound there, held still

and if it was enchantment, then I'll spell
it back: reach my hand behind the bar
to fix the woman, rearrange the chairs,
pin the charts of owls and woodland birds,
set that night's callers at their table,
make sure the fire is lit and in its place.
Then, cut a hole, shut one eye, peer in.

Sally Goldsmith

The Albion

The proportions of the Albion
honour the New Jerusalem's
in the Jerusalem of the North,
capital of God's Own County.

"A cold coming I've had of it!"
I opened with on my first visit:
"Well, it's not my fucking fault"
the Albion barmaid explained.

A railway pub where lines cross,
you cannot think inside this box,
a place for drinking religiously,
for silent prayer and meditation.

A trainset maker cast a template
of the Albion's cube in cardboard
for a fold-out model accessory,
the Platonic archetype of a pub:

but the Albion is more unique
than forms or monotheists' Gods;
it makes Mo's Bar feel undank
and warm the Slaughtered Lamb.

Yet its stout is black and comely,
shipped from Dublin not London,
blacker than the tents of Kedar
or the curtains of King Solomon.

Bearing King David's gold harp,
through its glass darkly, the light
separates as first at God's word
so on the face of my pint's head,

untouched, a host still below me
the colour of a new, thirsty page:
the Albion squares this circle,
and I drink to its alchemical ink.

Ian Duhig

Róisín Bán

The M1 laid, they laid us off.
We stayed where it ran out in Leeds,
a white rose town in love with roads,
its Guinness smooth, its locals rough.

Some nights we'd drink in Chapeltown,
a place not known for Gaeligorès,
to hear Ó Catháin sing sean-nós –
Ó Riada gave him the crown.

Though most were lost by 'Róisín Dubh',
all knew his art was rich and strange
in a pub we drowned in our black stuff
when we laid the Sheepscar Interchange.

Pulped books help asphalt stick to roads
and cuts down traffic-sound as well;
between the lines a navvy reads
black seas of words that did not sell.

Ian Duhig

The Name of the Name of the Rose

Among rose names, beauty seldom figures.
A small imagination's beggary
is guilty of *Parkdirektor Riggers*,
The Duchess of York, *Gertrude Gregory* ...

I used to drink in 'The Pub With No Name'
till they changed it to 'The Duchess of York',
so we rechristened it 'The Pub With No Shame'.
No good would come of it. There was much talk.

Both the pub and the rose after the divorce
were renamed, as if anyone cared tuppence.
While they were thinking up something worse,
we suggested 'The Arselicker's Comeuppance'.

Ian Duhig

The Eel's Foot

We've earned this pub, our annual reward
for heath and shingle, brambles, nettles, mud,
those sagging gates held up with bailer twine.
Some years it rains. The sea, our right-hand guide,
beat time along the sand bars till
we cut inland – the landmark sluice,
and swallows scooping deeper in the reeds.
Marsh harrier? Perhaps. A heron lifts
as slow as us. The wild plums are just ripe
beside the gritty hiss of ruffling wheat.

But that's the walk and here's the pub, its name
too known for puzzling at and, one year on,
a sun-warped bench, and other walkers –
a spread of maps, the salt of chips and Adnams.
The place to measure what's achieved.
Another year. This pint goes down a treat.

D A Prince

50p Gets You Four and Maybe

the Italian restaurant on High Street
turns back into James's
where every week I portioned out
my Saturday wages for bacardi and cokes.

Mr Jones plays first
and those of us who have it
agree that it's not the best song on the album
but the most upbeat

and that counts for something
on a Friday night in Worcestershire
and even fifteen years later I hear it
played in pubs

and find there's a type of man
in every bar
who likes everyone to know
that he knows all the words.

Stay brings out melodramatic gestures
from the sixth-form girls
with scary voices for the middle eight,
goth-pop fingernails and eyeliner

and if in a hundred years
I could put my ear to those beams
I'm sure they'd still vibrate
with the saxophone from *Baker Street.*

All the boys slap their palms
against the table for *Hey Jude*
Na na na na-na-na na
and some of them are doing it too hard

and there is so much flying beer
that it rises up from the floor
like the winter flood
and we're sent out into the walk home

with its kebabs, its civic flowerbeds
and sleeping geese
the fishermen waist-deep
enjoying the quiet.

Suzannah Evans

The Castle

The whole of time is happening at once
in the Castle Hotel, where Guinness
the pub cat dodders spittily from lap to lap,
Mad Friday workmen line the bar

and the rygbi boys are taking the Castle Challenge
a shot of vodka, three goes in the spinny chair
out one door, in the other for another shot
and three more spins, victory and respect

while I'm the first to admit love in the flat upstairs
to a man who keeps an old bottle of milk
evolving on the windowsill. When I get out of bed
unhoovered crumbs will stick to my feet.

Someone puts *Eric the Half-a-Bee*
on the jukebox, then *Baba O'Reilly,*
and we hold each others' shoulders
in a circle, ready to dance to the fast bit

while a lifetime's worth of passive smoke
billows from the upholstery
as the new proprietor rips it out
and stencils lyrics from *Angels*
by Robbie Williams all over the walls in pink

and no one wants to sit in the chair
that's shaped like a wooden hand
in case it grabs them
and won't let them go home.

Suzannah Evans

The Cardigan Arms

The Cardi's still there (but I never go in).
A body-less jacket embracing you
Or a washing line of woollies in the wind.

The oldies would sit on a green leather bench
Staring ahead, supping their brew.
The Cardi's still there (but I never go in).

The oldies moved; their houses have been
Pulled down. Sky TV now, though
Better than a washing line of woollies in the wind.

New Year's Eve: Joyce, the landlady, singing.
All pissed, none of us had a clue.
The Cardi's still there (but I never go in).

In the upstairs room there was dancing
A striking miners benefit 'do'.
More than a washing line of woollies in the wind.

Drinking, laughing, all for the asking.
Mild, bitter, friends we all knew.
The Cardi's still there. I'd never go in.
A washing line of woollies whistling down the wind.

Moira Garland

At the Bear

Havant, 1795

You are growing old ungracefully
as if you had never been young,

never welcomed Queen Victoria
who stopped with you once,

though you barely remember whether
she stayed – whether she was amused

or disgusted at the signs of your encroaching
shabbiness, or whether she just shook out

her heavy mourning skirts, blew her nose
into a lacy handkerchief, and went on her way.

And what about hosting Winston Churchill –
the way he drank Malmsey till the keg ran out,

then switched to Courvoisier, left nothing
behind but a trace of cigar smoke,

and a phlegmy cough to make way for
General Dwight D. Eisenhower,

who must have been chuffed to know Winnie
had drunk there, too. Your stair carpets

are threadbare under my feet today, sport
different patterns on each floor, the halls

the dining room, the snug. They're covered
in shapes too faded to make out: shapes

that could be floral or geometric, blurred hues
of gold, burnt-orange, bordello red, where each day

black canvas bags labelled 'clean' queue up
in the halls maids call out to one another:

Are ya' done there? Five's still asleep, again!
  Where are the bags labelled 'dirty'?

Whisked away earlier in grubby vans?
In the dining room your air is musty, ringing

with the clink of cheap cutlery. Croissants
curl up against one another in a sad plastic tower,

next to Danish pastries dotted with raisins like flies.
Do you still boast that your beams are made

from wood recovered from the Spanish Armada;
that the post up the road was the one where the last

dancing bear in England was tethered? And here
in this room I can't help but wonder whether the DNA

of guilty lovers still marks the counterpanes
of those too eager to turn the covers down first.

Wendy Klein

The Mermaid Inn

In the Mermaid Inn an accordionist
is playing *Les Flonflons du Bal,*
his fingers as green as the barmaid's scales.
Edith's white face hovers in exile –
no sadness now, we're the party next door
and *c'est chacun pour soi.* When he stops
pumps thud and measures click.
Scotch floods over ice like flame.

In the Mermaid Inn they give us masks
like Harlequin or Pulcinella. Our smiles
are fixed. The accordionist plays – this time
it's a drinking song and we raise our glasses,
hoping that joy's infectious, while the barmaid
laughs with eyes of stone. Her fish's tail
coils out of sight behind the bar. Alcohol
smudges our sight with warmth.

In the Mermaid Inn time's lost in liquor
that burns our throats with truth. We're dervishes
glimpsing Valhalla, touching its stone
with our fingertips. Its brightness seems
familiar. But at closing time
when music stops and lights are dimmed
we can hear waves crash on the nearby shore
and fishermen shout as a boat goes down.

Antony Mair

The Ship

A three-mile walk from home, up the hill to
the canal, where blokes with the blues or
shagged-out marriages sat with rods and
keep nets, hoping for a kill.

I used to go there with my father when he was
turning to a husk; sky fell on dark water,
reeds shook, lapwings rose and fell and
called out from the dusk.

I took you there when we were young, to
drink with our feet in the water. I wanted
you; I liked the thought that you were
someone's precious daughter.

Then my mum was dying and I went there
alone to sup. The landlord went missing
and some guy mimed sex with a pool
cue, his girlfriend doubled up.

The beer was John Willies's best, topped
with a tight, creamy crown; its golden
bubbles streaming up, when other
things were streaming down.

Lately, I went there with my oldest mate:
swans on the levels, locks restored, the
landscape of my youth overgrown, hiding
the places I'd haunted, bored.

Things were disappearing, I said. He said,
It's not over till the fat lady sings. I got a
round in, watched the lass behind the
bar soaping off her wedding ring.

It wasn't over yet, but things were
certainly moving that way: they'd shifted
the bar, moved the toilets inside, which
had been outside, back in the day.

Between the canal and its cellar The Ship
had a fabled sheet of lead rumoured to
keep the beer cool all summer, the way
a decent coffin chills the dead.

We drank bitter and I thought of you.
We laughed. There wasn't much to say.
We drank too long, we drank too much –
we drank to old times anyway.

Graham Mort

The Nursery Rhymes

On Queen Victoria Street,
in every face I meet,
in blasts of winter's breath,
I see the marks of age.

And adults know the rhymes
that once seemed comforting
are always about death.
The rings o roses seep.

In and out The Black Friar
is where the money goes.
In the pub it's piping loud
and warm as swaddling clothes.

They wet each head with drink
as if we could start blank,
forgetting Bloody Mary's
cockleshells can torture;

that the Muffin Man of Drury Lane
baits children to his shop;
that blackbirds will peck
the maid's nose off;

that bricks and mortar will not stay;
the dish will run away
and the Great Bell of Bow
does not know.

Here amongst the dregs
Humpty is a stone egg.
Brandy boiled with ale
makes you feel unbreakable.

Clare Pollard

Bitter

Béor, bor, ber, the bar taxidermy of pickled eggs, barred
for vinegar years, soaked centres munched among the sulphur
of Marston's top like a freshly-struck Vesta,
or malt reddening the Osset. Forget your nose, bookshelves
for the ladies and empty pub rooms, elusive as family:
sit the hours down with a Humpty's Fuddle,
white tip and tawny bulge, churning milky to settle.
Aromatic bitter wants to ferment in the Norwich area
and a loving, peppery ale, unsoured by life, seeks a tasty mat.
Avon's Gurt Lush WLTM a surprisingly attractive dentist
and Tring's Side Pocket for Toad WLT know if you can indulge a head fetish.
'I am from Yorkshire', boasts Salamander Mudpuppy, 'Are you local?'
'Look at these beer handles', opines Stoatwobbler and no drips Pot Wallop;
'I am a Greek God miniature', lies Brandon's Grumpy Bastard.
'I'll bake you a cake!' claims Barm Pot from Goose Eye
and Dark Side of the Moose is into music and cinema.
Oban's Fair Puggled wants frottage with a Cornish:
'I have a cloth-cap image, but please enjoy my gentle underpinning of hoppy
          bitterness.
I am an old ale with lactic sourness, but still lush and tart with sappy malt.
I am in love with a sottish idler, but nevertheless
feel free to malt my hopper, boil my wort, tun my storage,
oxygenate my sugar, grist my mash, grass my liquor,
sparge my grain, yeast my vessel and fine my rack:
if not, get lost with the droonkards in their nektar cups,
tapster victims among mazors of sack and Virginia tobacco,
most potent in potting a noppy ale
where Tetley glasses used to sail the air
changing the channel to random violence.'

Antony Rowland

Friday at The Moon

You're probably right, I look the type
who drinks vanilla lattes, but there I was
with a shot of something devastating,

and yes, I did entertain the regulars
with my slurred, cursive eloquence.
I probably sang. I probably chased a man

with a red rose between my teeth.
I tip-toed past the stone couple
who never talk to each other.

I tottered by Prosecco-fluted hens
saluted the old boy in last season's mildew
the Adidas man who speaks to his hands.

I saw pale ale ghosts. Lonely hearts.
Golf-kitted students necking snakebite
on a crawl they won't remember.

No idea how I got back, but if you said
I floated home on a magic carpet
who'd doubt it. I felt enchanted.

Did I look happy to you?

Maria Taylor

The White Horse Inn

You and your Robert Smith hair
idling by the cigarette machine,
me with my polka-dot top
riding high above my midriff.

Miles, the bland American
at one end of the bar,
the landlord at the other
selling vodka to girls.

Then there's the poor sod
we forgot, who jumped,
quite drunk, into the well,
still waiting for his applause.

The musk of your black denim
was like the air inside a crypt,
the taste of your hair was like
the taste of my hair, all of it

lit by gaslight. Your breath is scored
into the nicotine-stained walls,
your DNA in the flakes of skin
stacked between the flagstones.

The ghost of a fire sings
in the hearth, spectral carcasses
hang from the ceiling, the thirteenth
hook turned back on itself.

Sarah Stutt

Pub Crawl Prose

Quarry Bank Mashers

I grew up in Quarry Bank, a small town near Dudley in the West Midlands. There are many complaints these days about the decline in the number of pubs, but even then when I started drinking in the late 1970s people were saying that in the old days the high street used to have something like thirteen drinking holes (in a two-hundred yard stretch) and we were now down to about five, and that included the Labour, Conservative and Liberal clubs. There were still plenty of other pubs in walking distance, so there was easily a choice of around twenty. My favourite local was the Bull and Bladder, which took its name from the one-time abattoir next door. The pub had a small room on the left as you went in, a bar on the right, an off-licence hatch where people would bring their own jugs to be filled so they could drink at home, and a long back room with another bar and an upright piano. As with many of the pubs back then, the toilets were outside the main building, and they stank. The beer was Bathams bitter, and occasionally when I'd had four or five pints and the pub was emptying I'd get on the piano and play boogie-woogie.

There was a period of maybe two years when I'd go on Tuesdays with a friend into the small room on the left to join a group of middle-aged men who would sing songs, either the well-known, such as 'Delilah' and 'The Green Green Grass of Home', or what I assumed were local tunes. One refrain from the latter included 'and we'd dance and we'd sing / And we don't give a jot, we're a jolly fine lot', which was just perfect once you were under way. Google tells me that it's actually a folk song called 'The Ashton Mashers', from Manchester. In the original there are the lines 'All the ladies declare, that we are a treat, / We're the two Ashton Mashers from Back Preston Street', but we sang 'We're the Two Quarry Bank Mashers from down Chapel Street'. A song just for us. One of the rules of the evening was that to be considered part of the event you had to lead off a song of your own choosing. I can't carry a tune, but my friend had no fear and I learnt to speak-sing with him the introduction to 'I Left My Heart in San Francisco'. It begins: 'The loveliness of Paris seems somehow sadly gay / The glory that was Rome is of another day ...'

The group called themselves 'Tone and the Tone Deafs', recognition that Tony was informally the leader of the a cappella band. It was never quite the same when he wasn't there, and it was deflating when I discovered he drank and led singing at another venue on Thursdays, as if he'd been cheating on us the whole time. The evenings came to an end when he got a girlfriend. He did bring her to the pub once, which seemed to break some unwritten code, but his musical interest must have given way to other priorities and the weekly gathering fizzled out. I've not tried to sing in a pub since.

Steve Earnshaw

'Ship in a Bottle'

When I Land in Northern Ireland

When I land in Northern Ireland I long for cigarettes,
for the blue plume of smoke hitting the lung with a thud and, God,
the quickening blood as the stream administers the nicotine.
Stratus shadows darkening the crops
when coming in to land,
coming in to land.

What's your poison?
A question in a bar
draws me down through a tunnel of years
to a time preserved in a cube of fumes, the seventies-yellowing
walls of remembrance; everyone smokes and talks about the land,
the talk about the land, our spoiled inheritance.

Colette Bryce

Magi

Joseph was the Famous Grouse,
and the Virgin Mary, the Babycham deer.
Standing in for the sheep and the ass
were the Black & White distillery terriers.

The shepherd loitering shyly with a lamp
was McEwan's Laughing Cavalier
and the followed star was a golden Harp,
the swaddling cloth a Smithwick's towel.

Up on the walls where they hung all year
were Pio, Pearse and Johnny Walker
carrying whiskey, liberty and prayer;
gifts befitting an Irish saviour.

Colette Bryce

Houses That Used To Be Boozers

This town has its stark share
of repossessed dark lairs,
of houses that used to be boozers.
Where once we were drinking
we're now slowly sinking
in sofas the colour of bruises.

Ex-sawdust saloons
are now minimalist rooms
where every night somebody chooses
to rest their behind
and half-silence their mind
in a slow death of sweaty-necked snoozes
in a tap-drip of box sets and docs.

But these houses they used to be buzzing
they used be busting and splitting and spitting and ripe.
These places they used to be tasteless
they used to be graceless and legless and feckless each night!

Down lop-sided streets
fact'ry workers would meet
in these houses that used to be boozers.
They'd wash the week's slog
in the honey-dew grog
in their bawdy and dubious rouses.

Now ladies frizz hair
in the Glade Plug-in air
of these houses that used to be boozers.
So far from the funk
of the blood, sweat and spunk
when these houses were floozey-filled boozers.
When these houses were ringing with song.
And I long for the throng of that song when we thrived

in these dives with their ligging and frigging and dirt.
These hell-holes where black-hearted arseholes
would pour souls, then sing and kick heads-in till everything hurt.

Farewell Rose & Crown
for The Ship has gone down,
she's no more for rum-infused cruises.
The mad Horse & Dray
is not bucking today
he's muzzled as McIntyre muses.

And clatters of pewter
are taps on computers
in houses that used to be boozers.
Hum-drum sobriety
there's no society
houses that used to be boozers.

In cordoned-off hush
we are turning to mush
in these houses that used to be boozers,
we're fingering phones
and we're drinking alone
in these houses that used to be
houses that used to be
houses that used to be boozers.

Luke Wright

Beached

I gaze at a life beyond the fly
glued to the picture window

watch the trawler go down in flames
the waves pummel the rocks

see the chopper circle the bay
winch the crew to safety

in the evening the sailors roll
into the bar, ask me what I'm drinking

later I hear their husky voices
in the room next door, their heavy breathing

imagine them forcing an entry
as I light a candle, get stuck in the bath

chair wedged under the handle.

Angela Croft

terminus

Gare du Nord Paris

any city in the world it's the same
the central station the formergrand hotel
that's now a bar the lighting that switches
from decadent to seedy mood depending

and it's here they gather the shuddering halt
of lives who seem always to be trying
to leave but end up permanently stuck
to the beerworn leather and the wooden stools

they move so slowly it's hard to imagine
them at night after the bell has emptied out
the delayed the nearlymadeits
coming alive and dancing in an almost

clockwork stagger around the station entrance
like the toys you'd forgotten how to play with
that have their own life when you're no longer there
next time you see them throw a nod or half

a smile to them the ones pushed down
under the weight of the night they've had
the piss stained souls the lost ones who travel
to find themselves the broken the heartless the wronged

may they find their way home

Andrew McMillan

Gin Fizz

as the sun drops
in this latitude
at 4pm, it begins.

almonds, orris root:
irises and venus, return
to me. lemon peel, liquorice.

be russia's alexander. conquer
the ancients. the climate suits you.
grains of paradise tick time, marrow

marks, capillary fractures. coriander,
forever's residue. cassia. bless the next
customary behavior. cubeb berries

for immersion. is there
a psychic threshold
to the heart?

juniper, dim door jambs.
anjelica's blood tonic
for unhinging the night.

Greta Nintzel

The Drovers' Inns: A Goose-eye View

Cows from Carmarthen, geese from Wales
were driven to be London's meals.
How could we geese have tramped so far?
Because they sealed our feet with tar.
How it stung soles with gobs and blebs
then burned like hell in our cracked webs!

What did they see, our round goose eyes?
Greenways, farms with rival collies,
inns where men slept, below damp thatch,
trusted the dogs to keep good watch.
They took the London coach alone,
turned the dogs loose to run back home.

Kind barmaids fed those dogs, fox-thin,
who snuffed coach ruts from inn to inn.
The landlord's blade sliced breasts. Our white
plumes plumped his beds, let poor guests write.
By your fast roads our inns shine, spruce.
Where is the sign which shows a goose?

Alison Brackenbury

The Slaughtered Lamb

Castrating irons
above the bar –
one pair. A dart,

mid-flight,
suspended
in the deep-fried air.

Two pickled eggs
 – your eyes –
in a glass jar.

Your ears –
pork scratchings
on a stone floor.

Eat a lemon,
a full one,
for a free half;

for a pint,
pocket the 8 ball
in the roof of your mouth.

A jukebox
swallows your money
then plays dead.

A local
hammers a coin of the realm
into a turnip.

Into your head.

Simon Armitage

Mine Host

I had a name but they have swallowed it,
downed it by the pint. And I have swallowed
so much that I might give way. I might.

Tonight, I just contain myself. I go on
pulling ale and nodding Aye and Gerraway?
with one ear cocked against the margin
of a conversation, on the edge
of mild debate and brewing trouble.

I have the punchlines, the final say,
Time, gents. Sup up. It's Time.
And they subside, obedient, cowed:

I shepherd them unsteady, hold the door.
And someone might catch hell outside,
someone at home might come it, question
what's been spent, someone might wonder
what I buy one half so precious as I sell ...

I slam the bolts behind. I touch hands,
gently, with myself and rock and sing
I wish I loved the human race, I wish ...

I tilt my head, Yes, my good man? Yes, Sir
Yes? Yes? Sometimes it will not pass.
The juke box dies. A glass of rum and black
burns sanctuary and in my mirrors
in my bottles me and me

and my cathedral settles.
Then I bucket the fag ends and ashes,
wipe the bar and spread the towels;
I gather up the dregs and slops
and tip them in my special cup.

Ann Sansom

A Skeleton Walks into a Pub

Skeleton Man, you walk into a pub.
The bartender says: What'll it be?
You tap the pump
with the most colourful label:
Some hedge wizard
in an English field wassailing apples.
Down in one.
That's when the trouble begins.

Skeleton Man, you perform admirably.
You include all constituent parts expected from a night out:
drink, fight, chip tooth. The liquid runs down
the inside of your legs—nice touch.
It's just that each element should occur at intervals.
In your life, all things happen all at once.
Nothing spaced out, nothing unfolds. You're too neat by halves.

Martin Kratz

The Star

All the rings, those Olympic rings
of might-have-maybe,
pool their losses
to a dripping thread.

Beer mats torn to confetti
fill the ashtray's memory,
faces distorted
by the bottom of a pint glass

opening into foamy ways
and other such cliches.
Do you fancy another?
Make mine a pint

for the road un-takable,
the swaying road
with midnight hedges
of foxglove and pennywort,

a stream somewhere
over granite, a pure thirst
quenched, the road
now a lane chilling down

to a frost hollow,
where your lost voice fills
the bottomless glass of night,
breath spilt into stars.

John Wedgwood Clarke

Ship in a Bottle

You hope it's like a genie but it's more like a ship.
What's in this bottle is amazing as a ship's folded rigging,
as her nine sheets stowed neat (but longing to throw

themselves to the wind, flapping sting-wet rope-ends).
Amazing, how she sails from the liquid's doldrums –
a single, some doubles, straight from the bottle.

Amazing how she changes you – you're almost
still the person peering at this from outside, saying
'Just one', but the deck flexes under your feet

and you're back on your sea-legs, face burnt, lips cracked
with the years since you last saw land. Amazing how quick
she turns and you stagger. She flies in front of the wind,

sails laughing, full rig, every creak and crack of her
saying *this* is what she was made for. And you,
borne along like a whole crew, singing.

Ramona Herdman

The Priest

McDaids, Henry Street, Dublin

Let me go in that unclaimed hour
just as the bolts are drawn
and the glass-panelled doors creak open.
To sit there at the end of the bar
saying nothing, an old poet
lost to his words, while the barman,
a priest at his marble altar, eases
through the preparatory rituals,
lays out the cardboard coasters,
lifts a glass to the light.
Then maybe he'll clear his throat,
offer a few words – *If you're a betting man,*
I have a tip for the last at Punchestown
and this poet will lift his head,
recite some well-worked refrain
about faith and God and beaten favourites,
so the priest will turn, tap-off
the waiting pint, set it pristine before me.
And I will take it to my lips and pray –
every day should begin like this.

James Caruth

A Drink With Tom

When a summer shower chases us
into the tap-room of The Grapes,
he stands, flannels rolled above thin ankles,
like Lazarus come from the dead.
I'm Tom, he says though no one asked
and wipes his spectacles with his tie.

A woman in the farthest room
reads his future in the dregs of a glass.
Someone coughs. Another minute passes
unrecorded till he splits a beer-mat
with his thumbnail to write an epigraph in Greek
and underneath in blue-black copperplate –

There will be time. There will be time.

In the corner two men playing chess
look down at their feet.

And I think to myself – should I presume,

but he raps his knuckles on the bar,
calls another round for the room.

And I think to myself – how should I begin.

There will be time for revisions
and a hundred indecisions.
Time to compose a liturgy for these souls.
But he raises a long white finger
as the grave of his mouth opens –

No, that's not what I meant at all.

James Caruth

Valuation

My mother used to tell people
our house was a pub
in the eighteenth century.
I could see the cobwebbed crates

and woodworm-riddled benches.
Together among the pewter,
we believed in our public house,
conscious of the cavity beneath us.

My father, a true landlord,
would say to every visitor
as they got up to go and he didn't,
The door is always open.

One day a man with a measure
came to price the place for sale.
Pointing needed doing.
There was no cellar.

Paul Stephenson

Calling Time at The Bull's Head

The Bull's Head has gone. Now offices to let,
a bleak image on a 'lost pubs' website.
No mark on its old walls to say – here
my grandfather died his very Scottish death:
a whisky chaser undrunk before the heart attack.

I was never told the full story,
the pub falling silent in creeping realisation,
someone running down the road to my granny.
I do know she ignored the knocking;
sent my mother to identify him, took to her bed.

This was her shame: his corpse removed
through a pub's back door, their friends' pity.
An emptied bank account had meant uprooting
from Spanish heat, housemaids and orange trees
to land in this sooty town where he built trains.

My mother was his favourite, learned to like
being with him in the pub and how a drink
could ease homesickness, while Granny chose
to gulp her humiliation with bicarb. A good death?
That last pint sunk and the malt waiting.

Alicia Stubbersfield

The Passion Flower

I don't drink in front of the barman.
I don't shake his hand or lift the drink
to my mouth while he is watching,
for fear he will exclaim at the sight
of my hands.
How red he will say,
how almost black with the cold.
He thinks me rude but it's the
muteness in my hands.

When he has looked away
I take my glass and my change
to the small dark table.
I hear the big voices, pointing away
from thought, to speaking,
but I cannot talk.
I sit in the corner with my clenched
tongue and my tight, swollen hands.
I sit and I think of the single ringlet
and the green star of leaves.

I think of the meaning found for these things.

That the leaves are clutching hands of soldiers,
that the tendrils are the whips –
that the five sepals and five petals are ten disciples,
that the five stamens are the wounds.

That's what they say it represents.

Tara Bergin

Winter Warmer

Homework ditched, we hiked through snow –
it would've been me who'd suggested a pint.
We couldn't tell field from road from pavement,
all things being equal in that prettified tableau.
We chose the public bar – its small, uncertain fire,
sank pool balls, Burton ale, bitterness,
strafed the dartboard – no-one to witness

one succeed the other fail, no points scored.
Four pints down we wove home via the bridle path,
feathered branches vaulting overhead,
flakes still falling, melting on our necks:
brothers by birth ... now brothers of the heart.
Moonlight, streetlamps, eyes and faces shone.
Next day, though, the warmth of snow was gone.

Jon Sayers

Downtime

Impossible to soak in the high buildings
that line the Royal Mile while sober,
so, unlike most tour guides, I always say
if you just totter along, the real map
opens out, and thereby you'll cover more ground
which leaves me free to spend an inglorious hour

below street level, a dram with a clean finish
set fair and square on the table.
No stranger to these shady paths that turn back
on themselves, I resume the business
of letting you go, giving myself
this one last porous hour to distil
thought from thought, until I can at least agree
that what we can't bear suffers our loss.

Rachael Boast

Pub Crawl Prose
The Rise of the English Pub

> *'They goe ten times to an Ale-house, before they goe once to a Church.'*
> *Thomas Young,* Englands Bane: *or,* The Description of Drunkennesse
> *(1617)*

From the starting point for Chaucer's pilgrims—and thus arguably for English literature—through Thomas Young's complaint that it was 'too much frequented by yong and old of all conditions', to its prominent place on twenty-first century lists of 'what makes England "England"', the pub has played a defining role in English social and cultural life. It has done so over many centuries, and eulogies to its significance as an integral strand in the fabric of English society often accord a sense of timelessness to that role. But the place of the pub in English life is not timeless: it has a history.

Indeed, the term 'pub' only came into common usage in the nineteenth century, as a shortened version of 'public house', which itself was not used until the end of the seventeenth century. Before this time England's drinking establishments were described as three distinct institutions: inns, taverns and alehouses. [[The first two catered principally to traveling elites: they were part of the nation's transport and hospitality infrastructure. The alehouse was their humble relation, the forerunner of 'the local', offering a place of recreation to the common man and woman. But before the English Reformation of the sixteenth century they were not widespread; in the Middle Ages the Church acted as the focus for recreational life, which centred on communal drinking at Church sanctioned feasts and festivals. Protestant reformers balked at this blurring of the boundaries between the sacred and the profane, and after the Reformation merry-making was banished from the churchyard. The alehouse emerged to provide an alternative, and they sprang up in every settlement across the land in the later years of the sixteenth century. As they grew in number and prominence, they also attracted the concern of the authorities, and the seventeenth century witnessed a sustained campaign by Church and State aimed at curtailing the newly popular habit of going to the pub. This campaign ultimately failed, and we've been going to the pub ever since.]] There was nothing inevitable about this historical development. It involved a considerable struggle, but one from which the alehouse emerged across the sixteenth and seventeenth centuries as a key institution in England. In large part this was because it facilitated one of the most important processes of social bonding in that society: participation in a form of recreation that contemporaries called 'good fellowship'.

Decisions regarding with whom to voluntarily associate beyond the contexts of work and the home are central to the development of social bonds, social networks, collective identities and forms of community. Such communities can be structured by institutions—a medieval manor, an early modern parish, a modern school, a tribe—that necessitate practices of association that are relatively or even exclusively involuntary, but many more are forged through the active choice to spend time in the company of others. In an age before social media, or in societies and cultures with low levels of literacy that preclude engagement in networks of letter writers, physical co-presence and the availability of suitable sites in which to gather were essential to such forms of voluntary association. Voluntary association could take on a formal character—clubs, societies, religious congregations, guilds and unions—and historians have, of course, dedicated considerable attention to the formation of such types of purposeful interaction. But less formal, and especially recreational, practices of sociability are ubiquitous and arguably more important. Their informality, and their status as 'leisure', tends to mean that they are understood to be less purposeful, and less historically consequential. They have certainly received far less attention from historians. Yet some of the most potent bonds in any society, those that motivate people's decisions and actions, develop from choices made about with whom time should be spent informally, and for pleasure. The study of recreational sociability—of which alehouse sociability, or 'good fellowship', was one of the most regular and widespread forms in early modern England—reveals a great deal about the motivations and allegiances of historical actors, both individual and collective.

It was this connection between the alehouse and meaningful practices of social bonding that enabled the pub to overcome official hostility and to win its central place in seventeenth-century English society. It is a victory reflected in a relative decline of such official hostility around the turn of, and on into, the eighteenth century, as government came to grudgingly accept that place. Even the Society for the Reformation of Manners recognised that recreational drinking was largely beyond reform, and concentrated their energies elsewhere. The difference between an improved alehouse and a smaller inn became less distinct, and the term 'public house' began to emerge as an umbrella term for both. Larger inns, however, became grander than before, and the eighteenth century brought them into a 'golden age' in which they became an even more important focus of elite sociability. The 'improvement' of both alehouses and inns can be seen as part of a broader 'urban renaissance' in this period, in which both the number and range of establishments available as sites of recreational sociability in England's urban centres boomed. New commodities, most of which had become available in the sixteenth and seventeenth centuries but which began to be mass consumed in the eighteenth, also emerged. Coffee and coffeehouses, gin and dram-shops, tea and parlours might all be seen as forms of competition to the traditional intoxicants ale and beer and the sociable forum of the alehouse. Levels of beer consumption fell in the eighteenth century as the consumption of spirits and hot drinks rose. The 'improvement' of the alehouse may have been part of a desperate attempt to keep up with this growing competition.

In country towns and villages, and no doubt even in large urban centres, smaller 'unimproved' alehouses nevertheless persisted—sometimes referred to as 'pot-houses'—where there were no coffee houses to compete with, and where gin was often sold in existing alehouses rather than rival establishments. Domestic tea consumption may, though, have represented a serious rival, and diary evidence suggests that this was becoming an important feature of the round of recreational sociability, especially for women. Whereas in the formative century between 1550 and 1650 the alehouse had been associated by its opponents with political subversion, reckless prodigality, the breakdown of households, the transgression of gender norms, and indeed all manners of disorder, by 1750 a number of these connotations had migrated to other institutions. The coffeehouse was now the site of political disloyalty and sedition; beer drinking was a loyal activity. But much more so than coffee it was gin that had taken the heat off the alehouse. In his famous prints of 1750, William Hogarth depicted 'Gin Lane' as the place where poverty, disorder and transgression were rife. Its companion print, 'Beer Street', depicted an alehouse scene in which prosperous tradesmen and market women drank wholesome beer, and read from broadsides together. It was, in essence, a positive portrayal of 'good fellowship'. It is one that would have struck a chord with the 'good fellows' of a century earlier, but it would have seemed unimaginable to them that their recreational drinking could be held up in public discourse as a model of appropriate behaviour to be contrasted with the evils of the excessive drinking of the poor. It is an indication that the struggle for the legitimacy of alehouses and good fellowship had been a triumph.

Mark Hailwood

Extracts adapted from *Alehouses and Good Fellowship in Early Modern England* (Boydell and Brewer, 2014)

'The Regulars'

It's Our Dance

for Lorna

Every Sunday
I play Nina Simone's
'My Baby Just Cares for Me'
& with a different flower
in your hair every week
you spring out from the bar
& I leave the mixing desk
& we dance with our hangovers
yes we dance around the bar
& last week we ended up
outside briefly on Lewes Road
in the petrol hazes
& we even waltzed
out to the beer garden
& everybody smiles
when we dance together
to 'My Baby Just Cares for Me'
& for a few precious minutes
it's as if we have all swallowed the moon
& everyone is lighter
& the world not ever end

Brendan Cleary

Marina

& at The Marina in that gaudy bar
we were watching the light slip away
& you took out a page in your notebook
& doodled loads of shapes
after the walk talking about our dads
when I wanted to kiss you & touch you
& said the day I saw you naked I'd faint
as then we laughed about the car lights
like caterpillars over in the distance
at Rottingdean cliff heading somewhere else
& that white haze was zig-zagging
across the grey water & rusty poles
& the yachts & you noticed the reflection
of the slot machine in the window playing itself

Brendan Cleary

Sunday Afternoon

on his 7th pint of Strongbow
he pulls out his mobile
& flashes up a photo
of 'her' in skimpy gear
wearing red leather boots
so I pretend to be envious
& wish the clouds I glimpse
would float down & land
over these aching barstools
& in their softness the sublime
coated all my movements
& at the start of the end
graves never got dug
& lovers never went adrifting

Brendan Cleary

Gift

was my dilated pupils
gave the game away
or the smell
of Old Holborn
in my hair
& I'd worked hard
all of the morning
on the bar stool
with the Racing Post
just to bring you that flower
pink & incredibly rare

Brendan Cleary

The Quiz

I know I've been reading too much news
when walking to the quiz, beneath the neon lights of
a body massage parlor I read the words "bloody massacre"
and when I stop to look again, then again, my mind does
this thing where it checks and double checks itself

and thinks 'isn't the word "of" weird, surely "of" shouldn't
be spelt like that', and before I can think there's two men
walking past speaking English, of all languages, something
about a camel, which happens to be where this quiz is,
The Camel, an ex-pat pub near Fuxing Lu, a quiz host called Ned.

Is there are a sturdier name than Ned? A pint or two
then I look for the loo, the toilet – "to let" – but this one makes sense.
I come back to my table to this question: "Rank the following incidents
from the most people killed to the least people killed: The Utoya
Shootings, Dunblane, The Nanoor Massacre, The Passover Massacre.
         Four points available."

We get it right and we cheer. I walk back past the Bloody Massage parlor
listening to a man telling his girlfriend "well at least he says what we're all
         thinking.
it's about time we had a man in charge who wasn't..." but he's drowned out
by one of those lumbering road-clean trucks, spraying the road with water
playing the same warning tune throughout every city I've been:

it's a small world after all
it's a small world after all
it's a small world after all
it's a small   small   world

David Tait

Self Portrait with Son

Too much to say, I say this whole hilltop was abundant
with buckthorn and horses, mares trampling wiry
bramble from The Pheasant to Bellhouse, to stand at
the junction and wait for the Shiregreen wind to blow
through them, the way spring blows through a city, and
then you were born, and here we are, returned to The
Horseshoe, a game of darts, the sky falling in through a
derelict roof. Floorboards have begun to panic-flower
harebells, little bluish groupies you gather for the table,
as though you're not listening, but I know you hear it
all, all these things to say about love and letting go, that
it's possible to figure time in the damselfly, among the
glittering row of optics, that every flight the length of
the bar is a day gone, a day gone, whole months
counting a measure more or less of light, the way light
comes to imitate moving on. You take my hand and
only say have faith, and my heart is like a damselfly
caught under a glass, held to the sky, its bejewelled and
clamorous beating, beating

Angelina D'Roza

Scarf

I left it in the Malt Shovel in Lambourne.
You'd bought it for me at Machu Picchu
that time I was having the new heart valve.
I loved the blue of it, and the silver threads
running though it like traffic lines at night.
What I'm remembering now is its softness
and the way I left it after me in the pub.

Some punter picked it up. I watched him
wrapped in it at Kempton on Boxing Day,
Clare Balding interviewing him on TV
before the King George. 'Nice scarf,'
she says. 'Llama wool,' he tells her.
'Someone left it in the Malt Shovel.
Here's hoping it brings me luck.'

Michael McCarthy

The Vic

Early for the reunion,
I reclaim my old corner stool, look

in the mirror behind the optics,
and watch myself enter, singing Sinatra.

The barmaids smile, refuse proposals –
including marriage – and pull the pints.

He's amazed at my Coke, regards it as
witchcraft, some potion ringed by garlic

and wants it replaced. I politely refuse,
then he's off, talking to anyone who'll listen

till they, too, turn away, leaving him with
his only option: the door and the night.

Mike Di Placido

Famous for Fifteen Minutes

Lee comes in the taproom in the suit
he's had made specially. Yellow as a daffodil.
That's Leeds for you. Some silky stuff;
peg-top pleated trousers. Armani shoulders.
A turquoise shirt. Turquoise patent shoes.
No one ever laughs. It's beyond laughter.
Round-faced sandy Lee who worships Bowie.

Mal props up the other end, perched on a stool,
hunched like Jimmy Dean. Biker jacket,
on the back, a hand-painted wolf's head
in a beltbuckle halo. Running with the Pack.
He isn't nuts about Bad Company but loves
the album sleeve. Close mates call him Sabbath.

No one laughs at them. No one takes the piss.
How it plays out in other pubs
where they're not regulars I can't say.
This is their gig. They're famous here.

John Foggin

Snakebite

i.m. Helen Penfold, 1961-1999

Things are looking up. We've
found a pub where the landlord,
convinced by my smooth lies, your

proper breasts, will serve us snakebite.
He tips the lip of each pint glass,
froths in lager, pours cider and asks

How much blackcurrant, ladies?
You smile at him, murmur *When* –
we love how his hands shake

as you take your change.
We gulp like seasoned drinkers,
avoiding the stares of the old gits

with their bitter, their racing pages.
The drink hits the spot and
everything is funny. You nearly

take my eye out playing darts.
And at the Rec on the way home,
full of sugar and gas, we slump

on the swings we dared each other
to leap from as kids, jewelling
our palms and knees with grit.

We lean back under the night sky,
under all the stars we can't name,
we're full of how we'll leave

this dump of a town first chance we get –
how we despise the regular lawns,
the sagging paddling pools, we're

singing as we approach our road.
Today was hot, like the days,
buckling with laughter, we shoved

each other over on your drive,
the tarmac sucked at our sandals
and the ice-cream van played *Lara*

from *Dr. Zhivago*, too slow. Tomorrow
we'll feel sick as dogs. But tonight,
here, under a bright, full moon,

we're amazing, and as we hug
on my doorstep, I taste you,
kiss the snakebite off your lips.

Catherine Smith

The Set of Optics You Wouldn't Let me Buy in Portobello Market, September 1984

Remember how I fell in love with them,
how they glinted in the weak sunlight
amongst the tarnished soup tureens,
scratched fob-watches? My hand went out
instinctively to trace the inscriptions –
whisky, gin, vermouth. Oh that word, vermouth –
evenings in a silk kimono, louche, bohemian,
sipping a way of life. Rachmaninov.
I'd have fixed them above my desk
in my high-ceilinged study
with its polished floors, I'd sit on
a green and gold Lloyd Loom chair,
overlooking a lush jungle of a garden.
That glug of spirits – *ah, ah, ah* ....
My own private bar. Look, if I'd bought them
I'd have stayed out of sleazy pubs
and drifted round my Hampstead flat,
thin and mysterious; I'd have written
that trilogy of exquisite novels, I'd be
taking a call from my agent –
the film rights – megabucks,
darling, and when could we do lunch?
Remember how I fell in love with them?
My hand went out. Oh, that word. Vermouth.

Catherine Smith

Bar Staff

The midnight queue at the bar is ten years deep.
They are waving notes in a dream of significance,
but we only serve in a strict rotation no-one seems
to understand. This one will have lost it all before
the dancing ends – leaving the drink we've poured
in a doorway with lumps of a meal, he will come to
long after the spillage has been cleared wondering
how the night ended, who did this damage to him.

His stalling eyes are trying to see what's going on
beyond the ornate bar, but they will not catch us
stopping to drink – we only pause for the measure
of air to struggle through an optic or to indicate
to bouncers with a nod of the head which punter
is about to leave his body behind. In the street
outside, the light is crepuscular orange and a man
sways gently into it, stunned but intact for now.

Oliver Comins

I Was Talking With my Marvellous Man-friend

about our girlfriends with their friends and how it looks
so good the way they laugh together, like a dance you could
learn but not well; and how it's hard sometimes to believe
you could be worthy of time they could spend laughing like that

when I noticed he wasn't talking back. He had a kind of
yes-I've-thought-that-not exactly-that-but-close-enough
look, so I stopped looking for the mercy of regular trips
to the bar and the toilet and looked at him instead. He said that no-one

tells you how friendship is a mystery, like love, because that would be
to admit that the universe never promised us friends
but sometimes it's a thing you need to say out loud.
So I said yes, it was a mystery, how he was reflecting light

like a seventies space-funk tin-foil pearly king. What light was there
to reflect? It couldn't come from us, because we're extroverts
and our best enemies say we can only drain light from them.
Is it possible that our best enemies are wrong?

Tom Sastry

The Regulars

A Friday feeling, half-way home,
rain's drummed you off the motorway,
good news from London aches for telling,

the name and the picture halt you: a pretty horse
from a tale you recall, though you haven't read it.
Inside, strangers: of course you know them too,

not exactly expecting you, but not surprised
you've turned up, stand there indecisively wetting
the speckled carpet with excess drops. They nod,

their voices graze each other from bar and nook,
if the way's clear, they'll thrust a remark at you
or a carefully phrased look, before downing

tankards of barley, pints of amber and rust.
Feelings kept close to the chest, they openly
tender their views. Regulars, come out

for a laugh, some cheer, a warm word, at the inn
where there's always room and it's fine to loaf
on a rainy night, hear a stranger's news.

Marjorie Sweetko

Saturday Night

He joined me, uninvited, at the bar: a roly-
poly dietician, his fractured jaw half bowling-ball
size and black. Over soda and lime, he gave me
his hardline battery hen philosophy:
Eating an egg is like eating a piece of Hell.

And more: the dietician had seen the Devil,
once, stepping out of a painting dressed
in sandals and a straw hat. Not only that – the Devil
followed him home and for six months hen-pecked:
Why not do yourself in. A close call. Still,

he survived. He'd had worse: like the solid hour
locked in a freighter's cold-storage compartment,
slipping on frozen kippers. Only now
he sees faces by the roadside in weeds and flowers,
my own face falling, as he rose, and simply said:

We'll meet again. I'll know where to find you.

A B Jackson

Lauder's Bar

Sir Harry smiles from every wall.
Rain turns to sleet and falls
on three taxis planted in the rank.
A bus emblazoned *Glasgow via Reykjavik*
to the USA & Canada stands

empty opposite. Some bright spark
has amended a scrawled *UVF*
to *LOVE* in the gents' toilets.
Milling around, fake-fur coats
and shirts the colour of Opal Fruits.

Hands flare from various cuffs.
The papers are full of 'LUNAR ICE'
and far-out possibilities for life.
I'm smashed. There is no us.

A B Jackson

The Man with the Budgie on his Back

The man with the budgie on his back
walks, stooped, to the bar
and brings back a tray of beers.
His movements are slow, as if
he fears the budgie might leave,
but the budgie is fixed to his back
like it grew there. The man's friends,
two girls and a man, are laughing
but they are not 'budgie people'.
They approach other drinkers, passers-by,
offering the blue budgie as a gift
but the most they get is a smile.
The man takes the budgie to the loo,
then brings it back again. Nowhere
is there irritation on his face.
The budgie knows how to choose
and sits there, on the checked shirt
that it likes so much, looking round
at more people than it's seen before,
most of them looking its way.
The man's friends want to leave.
They head off down the street
slowly, with the man still stooped
and the budgie in place,
as if they'll always be this way.

Matthew Sweeney

Mackie

Remember Mackie, the undertaker's apprentice?
How he'd stand at the bar, never sit,
and tell us how he hated Mondays.
How the first week he worked there
he couldn't sleep on his back –
he imagined the dark in those boxes he varnished,
and how someone like him would nail together his.
How we'd look at each other and shake the head,
sliding him a small one as we left
to continue to the pub down the street.
We suggested college, or the priesthood.
How we talked about premonitions
when the news came in – the one
piece of Sputnik debris that fell locally
fell on his head, one midnight
when he'd stayed on afterhours.
How we took to the drink for weeks.
How we avoided his punk successor.
How we agreed he knew all about it now.

Matthew Sweeney

My Friends, The Poets

My local knows I write. Every proper pub has its share of characters;
the bloke shot by the Taliban, the girl who fell asleep having sex in the
        toilet.
We're not the chattering classes, more gossip and dirty jokes.
Cockney, Yiddische, Gammon and Yard is the well I dip my pen in.
We like a turn of phrase, an inventive curse, when somebody says nothing
but everything. The up themselves and the bore we've no time for,
yet there's a true appreciation for the form. I'm often asked about poets,
Luke Kennard, Ian Duhig, Clare Pollard ... do I know them? What are
        they like?
The library takes a hit, and there's a second appreciative read
when my reply is, "you'd love 'em, they're a scumbag just like us."

Tim Wells

Your Shout

A vaping vicar and his West-end boyfriend
lift their Merlots to the light to look for sediment,

a train vibrates like a stomach complaint.
The roof shakes, someone quips, 'Are you there Sidney?'

Soaks in cravats, salt themselves away with Bacon,
'Dear Motherfucker of a man, how I miss him!'

Black cabs pant like loyal dogs
at the hems of the London dusk.

Divorcees from the working week loosen their nooses,
kick their old kit bags under the tables.

Beneath a promising sign, 'Be courteous to our neighbours,
show 'em what a good time looks like,'

you propose me as your literary executor, though
only your dreams are widely published; and you are married.

A barman with an accent like a butler who has turned tables
on his masters, calls time on the city.

There is still an hour to kill between the platforms
of an action and a consequence.

Miranda Yates

Bars

A woman walks into a bar. Her breasts are prominent
because of a hidden harnessing contraption she has on
under her shirt. Her spine cants from the strain of balancing
on stilt-like prostheses under her heels. Also, there is paint

on most of the skin of her face, layered up to a powdered
slick, picked out here and there in a stark play of lineament
across several of the frontal features, in black and red
and spectral blues. Nonetheless, despite such confinement,

she looks quite natural, and moves with surprising ease.
I say moves—it's more like staggered modulation, one
foot then the other providing the load-bearing fulcrum.
At rest, she eschews the tall stool. Momentarily, her eyes

flash out from the shadows in the mirror on the other
side of the bar—although whether by slip or by strike
I cannot ascertain. I nevertheless resolve to offer her
a drink—but do not know her preferences and don't like,

in these stagey, exposed, circumstances, to trouble her
with the burden of any direct approach. In the event,
I order double entendres and give her one. She doesn't
decline, but barely touches it. Watchfully, I sip the other.

Decades later, I see she is less glamoured, flatter heeled,
largely unpainted, although her hair has been piled
up into a lacy carapace. A fussy effect, but I'd recognise
her anywhere. Her telling self-halation, her lit-up poise,

seems undimmed. Shortly after that she is dead. More
paint is needed, a professional job, this time on my tab.
I'll be claiming it back, on probate. The barman calls a cab,
starts cashing up. I drink up and leave. I walk into a bar.

Andrew Lambeth

The Barrel-Dance

For a year I lived over a pub.
Monday and Wednesday mornings
I worked with half a mind, my ear
attuned to the traffic's rumblings
in the street, awaiting the warm beat
of an engine idling below:
the brewery wagon. When it came,
the world opened and I was at the window
to watch the new barrels unloaded –
not your spry aluminium kegs
but all the dead weight or iron hoop and wood
stave, and about nine gallons of beer:
a weight that if one of them took
a sudden drop it could crush a man's foot
and crack the paving-stone under it.

The driver would climb up over
the tailboard, sing out for the landlord
and then with a roll and a toss
spring the first barrel over the side
of the wagon and down to his mate
who'd catch it as it fell
with a thud that shook the building
on a coconut-fibre pad at this feedt
and spinning the cask on one rim
skate it towards the cellar
like a weightless dancing-partner
and juggle it horizontal to roll down the chute.

I thought no dancer or acrobat
could match the rhythm of their work,
their art of weight and movement,
but like all performing artists
they improved the world not a jot:
I never drank in the pub,
for the landlord remained a churl
and the beer in his glasses warm and flat.

Grevel Lindop

Ye Olde Trip to Jerusalem

It's like being inside an ear, or a hive. Wax-
coloured tunnels wind away into the rock.
This room's a bowl scooped from porous stone,
but for that oddly physiological
crevice going up to a cobwebbed height
lost in darkness above us. Centuries
of iron-hooped hogsheads have inscribed
those perfect circles deep in the walls.
The Castle's overhead:
once the Ducal Palace, smashed apart
and set on fire in 1831
by a mob demanding Reform. Now
it's Art Gallery, Regimental Museum, Beer Festival.
Down here, it's all so familiar:
the dusty black wrought-iron trim fiddling
along the front of the bar; the sticky table
that keeps on wobbling, despite
the folded fag-packet someone's carefully
wedged under its foot. And those voices –
their subterranean hum and echo. In the next room
some bloke rat-arsed from a funeral
or a wedding's trying to sing: 'And did those feet ...'
This place was old when Chaucer began writing.
It's where someone – crusaders, was it,
or pilgrims, I can never remember –
set out on their travels. Not us, though.
Make yourself at home, I'll buy another.
Surely we're at the exact centre of England.

Grevel Lindop

Parish

Imagine, the most thievish in the shire
with its clusters of blind ale-houses, home
to vagabonds and rogues. In one of these find
Francis Bland, pauper, common quarreller
and brawler, supping there, his clipped coin
spent on ale instead of shoes; or think up a brew
of dark souls setting out with swords, daggers,
pitchforks, staves to break down fences,
breach ditches dug round new enclosures,
drive cattle back to graze the common land.

Then think of us today. Quiz night. Drinks
are on the winning team, a chequered crew
of off-comers and locals – architect, mole-catcher,
teacher, lengthsman. This time their coin is good.
There's talk of the euro-zone, its sleight of hand,
bent politicians, bankers. Sedition's in the air.
But there it stays. Broken fences there may be,
stray stirks to deal with. But poachers, rustlers,
diesel thieves, they're from elsewhere, up the road
in Keasden say, Blackburn or Lancaster.

Mike Barlow

Masterclass

He never tired of explaining from his stool
the route to an immaculate Guinness.

Tilt your glass at forty-five degrees
to kill the splash. Hold it close

to the spout, avoiding contact. Take the brew
three-quarters up, then leave to settle.

What's done next is the barman's choice.
I liked to guess who he'd escort to the gents –

the young drag queen? The bear?
Toot like chalk on the black lid,

his eyes impish as he crept back to his squeeze
for hugs or squabbles. I'd get yanked in

to arbitrate, to remember whens and hows
while I tipped piled fag butts into bins.

The last time he left abruptly, before I could try
my fancy Shamrock, the stale heat relieved

by a blast of salty air. He never worked out
who he caught the virus from

and he didn't end his final class
with the ideal ratio of white to black.

Twelve years on, I haven't stopped waiting
to finish pouring that pint.

John McCullough

Two Halves
for Rupert Loydell

We enter the pub and I flick the switch
from New-Man-Dad to Chelsea fan.
In the other bar they've Sky on a giant
screen. We're two-nil down to Leeds, away. The pitch
looks terrible. You chuckle into your Heineken.

OK, so I'm not the man you thought I was.
But I need this half hour of mindless escape
just as much as you need that pint.
Mine's a half, if that's all right. Yes, it's because
of the time. And yes, I do know they're crap.

It's got nothing to do with logic and everything
with being seven in the last year they won something.
You either understand that or you don't.
I pity you because you just can't see it. Or won't.

Anthony Wilson

Sunday

The rain lashes down like a TV's static
as smokers huddle under pubs' lintels –
from the Lescar across to Porter Cottage
the storm turns from drizzle to dismal.
Bless he who, with the cool persistence
of a craftsman, re-rolls a soggy Rizla;
opening the botched attempt in silence
as he rolls it into another.

When you leave with her, the sky has cleared:
a van trundles down Sharrowvale past
the shell of a butcher's, boarded and barred;
the sun and bulky nimbus in weird contrast
as you open up the Marlboros, offer her one,
struggling to recall if it was accident or arson.

Ben Wilkinson

The Red Lion

Each Sunday afternoon the rugby team
came in and sang their songs, and filled the bar
with sweat and noise, shoulders and voices too big
for the room. My sister knew each one of them
by name, poured their drinks before they asked,
told them to keep their eyes to themselves, that if
she caught them looking at her little sister ...
I moved through that pub like a ghost, glided past men
averting their eyes. Some made towers of glasses
for me to carry, a thin and stinking baby
made of dregs, or lined them up for me to lift,
four in each hand, fingers damp with beer.
My feet ached from the sensible shoes, I thought
I looked a boy in the blouse, the knee-length skirt,
my hair tied back and pinned. She sent me out
again and again across the paisley carpets,
into the smoking room, where the noise was a roar
when the door opened and the air was thick and grey.
On my face, the hot breath of the washer,
its dragon hiss as the door was opened, each glass
burning its circle on my palm as I reached
to place it on the shelf. Watching my sister
tilt the throat of the glass to form the head,
or reach behind her, a double shot for a single,
the gurgle of the bottle as it refilled.
At 5 she sat down at a table and waited for me
to finish, smoked cigarette after cigarette,
men bending their heads to hers, passing light
and fire between them. She poured herself
a drink as the men made her laugh and she
was one of them but not of them, my sister
with black hair and olive skin and a laugh
like a cough and no fear or patience or love
or so I thought back then, when I was young
and stupid, when I stood behind her, waiting.

Kim Moore

Tuesday At Wetherspoons

All the men have comb-overs,
bellies like cakes just baked,
rise to roundness. The women tilt
on their chairs, laughter faked,

like mugs about to fall, cheekbones
sharp as sadness. When the men
stand together, head for the bar
like cattle, I don't understand

why a woman reaches across, unfolds
his napkin, arranges his knife and fork
to either side of his plate. They're all
doing it, arranging, organising, all talk

stopped until the men, oblivious,
return. My feet slide towards a man
with one hand between his thighs,
patience in his eyes, who says you can

learn to love me, ketchup
on the hand that cups my chin,
ketchup around his mouth,
now hardening on my skin.

Kim Moore

Pub Crawl Prose

The Buffet Bar, Platform 1, Stalybridge Station

As soon as you enter, you know that the journey was worth it. This is a place that feels both a little too good to be true and inescapably, quintessentially northern. Cosy lighting in the bar parlour, antique and mysterious railway bric-a-brac and memorabilia to lose oneself in, conspiratorial corners for secret assignations, a walnut bar to perch your novel or the crossword, at the end of which, under glass, glistening home-made hot pork pies, Eccles cakes and Victoria sponges. There are several real ales with enticing names, reeking of industry and Norse myth, a row of bottles of Vimto, and a tureen full of steaming broth 'freshly made'. The kindly, elderly lady ahead of you at the bar is greeted by name and with her usual, a hot elderflower cordial, at which point you think this is definitely too good to be true, or that I am a fantasist, or both. But no.

The lady served, her cordial carried away in a china mug, the barman turns to you to speak but pauses, noticing that the young serving girl has left the kitchen radio on and Heart FM is leaking through into the bar. 'Let me turn this rubbish off, sir ...' he begins, giving you a quick, appraising glance as he does so, at your book, your man bag, your smartphone ' ... and now can I say that, as you don't seem to be here for the steamy movies or the knitting circle, are you a card carrying member of CAMRA?

You are none of these but you are intrigued, and the barman can tell. 'Let me explain. First, a drink? A pint of Boltmakers? Named after our head brewer's local, The Boltmakers Arms in Keighley. "'I'll tell you now and I'll tell you briefly, I don't never want to go to Keighley'", he drawls in Salfordian, quoting the great John Cooper Clarke. 'Nice little pub. Oasis sponsored the pub football team for a while I believe. Now, let me tell you what's going on here tonight.'

Steamy movies is the humorous name given to the weekly showings of old black-and-white steam train footage in the back bar. He indicates a group of men of a certain age in caps and anoraks, some with pipes, which makes me think of David Hockney's sage observation that no pipe smoker would ever have road rage. One raises a cap in salute, increasing the sensation that I am in some kind of Lancashire Twin Peaks. 'The knitters are through there,' and he points to a clutch of women of varying ages taking needles and multi-coloured yarns out of carpet bags and with a variety of drinks in front of them: spritzers, tea, halves of mild. Other regular attractions advertised on the pub's crowded wall include Laurel and Hardy night, a poetry reading and several quizzes.

Next to them is a menu upon which my eye falls hungrily. 'Now then, sir,' the barman begins apologetically, 'if you've come for our infamous black peas' – this is a northern delicacy, often enjoyed around bonfire night and delicious in a Dickensian sort of way – 'then I have to tell you that they haven't really been soaking for long enough yet. I can offer you a hot pork pie from Saddleworth and mushy peas though, and after that perhaps some home-made pudding.'

'Yes, that would be marvellous,' I answer weakly, the evening beginning to take on the quality of a dream. On the wall a sign reminds me that this has been voted CAMRA's pub of the year. I'm just surprised it isn't every year.

Stuart Maconie

Pub Crawl Prose

Settling

I'd thought it must be the black February cloud on the tops or gluten in the beer. It's Gareth. Twenty-five going on sixty. He sits at the end of the bar rolling. Strands.

Last week he did a job for me, humping desks and cabinets up the old barn stairs into my new office. Unless I go and sit in the lounge with the lunch time pensioners, there's no way of buying myself a beer without his I don't mind if I do ...

He sits there with his little blonde beard, and his earring, rolling nothing, he licks, rolls, squeezes, adds another pin to the line on the bar next to the pint I bought him, folds down the pouch, presses the seal closed. Tuts a little pause in which I kick myself for not getting away quick enough. As I was just saying to –

Piece work. Gareth cleans the pub and is done by eleven. I sit in my new office up the road and am down here at two. We're the Northern Powerhouse Gareth and I.

* * *

Today is Gareth's day off. Gareth sits one end of the bar with his baccy and papers, and Cath sits the other end of the bar with her vape kit and Silk Cut.

If someone wants a short that's not on an optic Renata pauses a second to locate the shelf. Gareth doesn't say anything, just points with an expression on his face like, Where do they find these people? Cath tuts a little cough at him each time. Sometimes she will say, Give the poor girl a break you fucker.

Cath only calls Gareth a fucker when she is this side of the bar.

As it is their day off I decide to show some imagination and order a double gin and slimline. At the bar I nod at Gareth.

He says, Now then.

I say, Alright [Fucker].

And he says, I won't say no.

Then, As I was just saying to Cath ...

* * *

I know I have become a regular when Chris the landlord draws the heavy curtains across the front bay and asks me what I'm having.

It's on the house, first one.

Gareth has told me about the legendary all night lock-ins but the chances of tonight being legendary are slim.

I'm regretting not choosing a short.

I stand, floating, bloated, wishing I'd left three hours ago when there was still an evening, set off across the room for the bogs.

I think the lights going out must be a lock-in, but Gareth says, I'll sort it boss, puts down his ale, tucks his rollie behind his ear and heads for the cellar door. We hear the soft slump, hard knock and whimper and everyone looks.

Cath says, What's the fucker gone and done now?

Renata stands three Peroni glasses tucked in her arm, one half way to the shelf.

Chris cocked on the pump, waiting for my head to settle.

For a second, even though The Midland is exactly half way between the east and west coasts I can hear the sea, and as Cath sets off to peer down the cellar steps I imagine her running to the cliff edge and put my hand on her elbow to stop her.

Steve Dearden

'A Parting Glass'

All the Pubs Where We Used to Meet are Sinking

The Little John is up to its knees,
The Lowther shoulder high,
The Kings Arms just keeping its head.

In The Bonding Warehouse, the barman
snorkels to collect empties
and only fish remember what we said.

At The Cock and Bottle barstools are afloat,
banging against the window I looked out of
when you asked how I'd been and I lied.

Carole Bromley

A Parting Glass

and when they sat together,
the older brother and the younger,
without the landmass of the others,
the busy harbour and the open field,
there was a feeling like the welling
of a shoal of fish about to surface,
about to flash their shining selves
or snatch the air, a promise
that was fluid, solid, here and now

Maura Dooley

He Buys Her a Hot Whiskey

Of all the things
to make me feel
it was no dream:

a glowing glass,
your sense
of audience intact,

molten, lucent,

this was it.

Maura Dooley

Water and Weight

We toasted near Monk's House, the South Downs
weaving a spell around us. *Let's keep
the rocks out of our pockets for as long as we can.*

Virginia knew about heft and the pressure
on an hour, a day. The writing room held
but was flimsy in tidal winds, letting in salt

and the moon-chased confusion of grief.
The steady stream of words, good company
would fail. What communion she sought

was with water and weight. We bought
another round, said *cheers, slainte mhaith
mud in your eye.* Not goodbye.

Linda Lee Welch

From The Other Side of The World

1. The Bucket of Slop

I look back at those evenings in *The Bucket of Slop*
with fondness and a heart soft as warm butter

I remember Elsie behind the bar with arms like hams
and breasts like other hams and a knife instead of a tongue

I remember the sawdust on the floor and I remember
wishing they would change it sometimes

I remember my friends, and some people I had fights with,
and wonder where they are now, and if they are still alive

2. The Wicked Wench

I look back to when I took over *The Wicked Wench*
and tried to keep out the hoi polloi and improve its customer base

I remember converting the pool room into a restaurant
and importing Pierre the chef from Provence

I remember discovering he was an alcoholic womaniser
who didn't know one end of a chicken from the other

3. The Thirsty Frog

I look back at proposing to Trixie in the snug of *The Thirsty Frog*
and the way she looked: out of her depth

I remember how the walls shimmered romantically in the candlelight
because Ron the landlord was trying to cut his overheads

I remember everyone drinking to our future good fortune
and not realizing I was going to have to pick up the tab

I remember thinking that it's times like this you never forget
and however hard you try you know you won't be able to

4. The Stack of Hay

I look back at the night somebody burned down *The Stack of Hay*
and wondering where we were going to hang out now it was gone

I remember thinking it was our second home and better
than our first home because you didn't get moaned at there

I remember realizing that to walk another half a mile to *The Soft Touch*
would mean having to stagger an extra half mile home

5. The Other Side of the World

I look back at the motherland from the other side of the world
and know there's nothing anywhere like an English pub

I remember thinking that one day I would be asked to write
in celebration of the English pub and wouldn't be able to do it

I remember the different periods of my life and how there's a pub
that springs to mind for each one, a pub with memories attached

I remember how I would not so much want to celebrate the pub
as simply thank them for being there – but perhaps that's the same thing

Martin Stannard

The Royal Oak, The Wallingford Arms

The Royal Oak, The Wallingford Arms,
The Prince of Wales, The Fleur de Leys,
The (new) White Hart, The Wheatsheaf –
ill-lit, unwelcoming and dirty,
the public houses of my youth.

Small tables, chipped-Formica topped,
ashtrays, unemptied, battered tin,
and beer mats advertising beer,
a glum reminder that in towns
like ours only women drank wine.

Now and then one would become
'Under New Management', and all
the regulars would be banned
for a week until, starved of trade,
they'd be let back, grudgingly

by the landlord and his lady wife
who'd last a year or two, before
they left to run a bar in Spain.
Too young to drink they let us drink
till ten, but locked us out of lock-ins.

Jonathan Davidson

Poem

I wanted to cross the tidal river
by means of the ford the Romans found
and stumble up the shingle beach
to a new life on the northern shore.

And I wanted to have passed halfway,
midstream, drifting, a man heading south,
taking in water but likely to make it,
his heart set on seeing the turf maze

and buying a drink in the isolated pub.
And I will see him gather up my life
like a number of stacks of small change
stood on the mild- or bitter-puddled table.

Jonathan Davidson

The Night is Young

I have drunk
a highland malt that took my head off
to show willing at two in the morning,
the odd glass of red with a meal for my heart
and a pint of shandy at the quiz,
but not
let my hair down sick as a dog
hair of the dog, not drunk drunk,
not for years, and even then, hormones
everywhere, never lost it completely
brought back a curry in a taxi
on a girlfriend, not said
what I didn't know I meant it was
the drink talking
not Friday night drunk or office party
drunk in charge of a photocopier.
Let's have some fun
as Jane Austen said
on this reckless planet.
God help me to get to this age
and never what a great night that was
if only I could remember it
completely and utterly
drunk? Me? Not ever,
not yet.

Peter Sansom

Clemency for the Drayman

They all ended up the same way, of course,
deep in the silt and swirl of the Thames,
its seeping into black earth,

that tilt of the great maned head,
the jawstretching roar, skulls tumbling
to settle in a mulch of scree and rotted leaf.

Here, the driver of the brewer's dray
hauling on the reins of the scurried horse,
tasting blood on his lip and not knowing why;

there, the king in his Tower
hearing the lion rage at the bilious sky,
wondering at the grime of clay on his tongue;

and the lion itself, crazed and mean,
pacing out time in bars of light on stinking stone;
the ghost of him.

It's the lion we remember.
Watch him catch the sun, the glint on the river,
the glint in his painted eye as the tide turns.

No one will recall the ale spuming
sweet with herbs and hops from barrels
flung across the strand

or the rearing horse, the spooked horse,
clattering away as if nothing would catch him
but the wind.

Jane Lovell

Pub Text from The Royal Inn on the Park, Hackney.

I bought another dress that I would like to take
off you from a shop on the canal, 'Hip Vintage',
old words for second hand's as good as new
and age is not a style disadvantage.

It's summer silk, low cut. Couldn't resist
you in, half in and not really in it.
Weird, given we've split up, I'm half-pissed
and not even sure, like us, it will fit.

Button-un-, job-done barfly youths, fizz smiles,
hearts on sleeves and clothes worn so retro,
can't yet know the width of bedrooms, the miles
of vast ceilings asked *where did the time go?*

I drain another pint, frilled petticoat whites—
bottoms up! To old, ambitious transvestites.

John Fennelly

Wedding Reception at The Brill and Grouse

Raise a toast for the bride and groom
Rake a tobacconist for the bridge and groper
Rally a toccata for the bridle and gross
Ramble a toddler for the briefs and grotto

Ramekin a toehold for the brigade and ground bait
Ramp a toffee for the bright and groupie
Ramraid a toggle for the brill and grouse
Ranch a toilet for the brindle and growbag

Ramraid another toggle for the Brill and Grouse

Cheers!
          Chairs!

Chores!

Pam Thompson

After Closing Time
for Joe

We head to the edge of town,
to the black river and old stone bridge.

Two boys full of vodka,
tipping side to side like flames.

And for a laugh, we climb
the railing and hang from our arms.

Below in the deep, two boys
peer up at us over their feet.

Like drops of water
we are gathering ourselves to fall.

One of us says, *You go first*,
and we echo this back and forth.

We are here for a very long time.
Years in fact. I marry. Divorce.

You skip all that, become a father.
We see less and less of each other.

Now we are what the world
considers 'men'. Which is to say

we've learnt that falling is inevitable.
Yet here we are still, side by side,

two boys way past closing time,
holding on until the other lets go.

Mark Pajak

On the Third Day

For my twenty-first we did the Mumbles Run,
a pint in every pub on the Mumbles Road
between Blackpill and Limeslade. Brains
is the local brew. It's easy to see why.

The limp evening drizzled over the city
sodden paper settled on the pavements.
No one was pretending apart from the statues
and we didn't recognise the statues.

Graham showed me, on an earlier occasion,
the art of drinking beer. You don't swallow
so much, you pour it down. If you have to swallow
take really big gulps, much bigger than you think.

The station was nearly empty, the last train
had left and he was on the platform opposite,
crouched over but unable to call out
hesitating before that moment.

Don't worry you won't drown. I could down a pint
in NINE gulps, Graham in FIVE and Tony in ONE

his heart beating inside a stranger's chest
his eyes gazing out from a stranger's face.
It was probably too late to save him.
A dog barked in the distance.

Some people came late and joined us halfway.
I didn't realise you could do that.

Cliff Yates

A Drink at the Door

As I had asked for a night-light, the chamberlain had brought me in, before he
left me, the good old constitutional rush-light of those virtuous days ...
    – Charles Dickens, *Great Expectations*

That's what I'm reading here. I mean the Dickens.
That and some downloaded contemporary
I keep switching from, on my lighted Kindle.
But it's not the light that came with this reader
and candles the cold, framed screen; it's the trick
of the light in this pub that detains me.
And not in this place alone. What is it
this yellowed, well-thumbed light has borrowed from?
By a less lonely table, a dog's ear
twitches. Somehow the glow pooled round my pew
hosts its own table talk. As mahogany
is a wood of a certain age, so too
this light is dated, refracted by it
and the dark matter that's caked in the grain.
And it's refracted, beyond that, by smoke
at the back of this malt, death and life mixed,
as familiar as a browned penny,
particular as fog. And it picks up
a dim street in Dickens, a door that gives
to this light, refracted here by the din
and the sharp bark of that dog. The Bear.
That was it. Dad's early haunt. Those big doors
that looked locked. And there, ensconced, hours later,
the same filament in frosted, smoked glass.

Like a burr stuck in the folds of my scarf,
this light has trailed me longer than I knew.
Out there, the darkness also has a hand
in these refractions. That and the bitter
cold I'm in from. If I keep losing you,
please bear with the thought of light. Like this shot
of malt bears its long, peat finish, sea-noted, late ...
There's a low fire breathing, and an argument
somewhere. And I've come to an inn. In Orkney.

1824. In his Irish burr,
I hear the landlord attempt to intervene.
Four generations later, his descendent
pokes at the grate of his pub in Aberdeen.
And his wayward daughter asks for a light
in a Midlands asylum, home for life.
And her daughter, between trains, wanders out
to Needless Alley, looks in at The Windsor,
catching the eye of my eventual father.
Shortly they'll see, in this same light, they share
the one brand of cigarette.
                          The refractions
will go on, past my stay; I'm only here
for one. A drink at the door. A last drop
trails down the glass. I'll pack my Kindle away.
Exit this light that has taken me in.

Zaffar Kunial

Digits

The Pete Townsend windmill
shattering a lampshade
made of thick glazed pot
when I was drunk and eighteen
was a near thing.
Had the tendons not been
re-joined, what I'd have missed most,
now I think about it,
are the two that I pressed
into the frog-slack spot
under the jaw of a man
whose heart had stopped,
holding them there
for ten long seconds, searching
for a carotid throb.
Nor could I have coaxed rock 'n' roll
from a gut-strung acoustic
at that party where
we watched from the decking
as the sun ran its fingers
through the buzz cut
of a lawn, the chords
inspiring a raft of dawn survivors
into bird-startling song.

Roy Marshall

Probably Not the Best Summer Job in the World

Leave the sun to blaze on foyer doors,
scuff up stone steps, change into pink shirt
kipper tie, purple suit with wide lapels

climb behind a Perspex box, sell tickets
with grubby fingers, hand over Maltesers,
pop-corn, hot-dogs, ices

get caught mid-impression by the manager,
an imitation of his voice hung like a jammed
frame in his stare,

mooch and ghost with dilated eyes
through drifts of smoke, blasts of *Pearl and Dean,*
muffled sobs, roller-coaster screams,

find lovers joined at the lips after the credits
have rolled, glide a banister to catch Michelle Pfeiffer
before she turns into a hawk,

exit via the fire escape to meet you for a quick pint
between shows; apart from this last, no, I don't wish
I was back there, since you ask.

Roy Marshall

A Run Out to Zennor

There are three things about the Tinner's Arms:
firstly, the extra blue waxed twist of salt
in the bag of crisps that time; second, how bats

appeared out of the gloom, skimming our hair
when, bored of adults, we took the sunken path
to the cliff, how we screamed back to safety,

to the bench-and-table combos bleached by rains,
to yellow lights, our paper straws chewed flat
in empty Vimto bottles; third, Morveren

luring Mathey Trewella with her song,
how they dwelt, him blue-lipped, her all muscle,
down among black rocks where barnacles cling,

living on jelly anemones, silver darlings.
A fourth thing I learned later is DH Lawrence,
newly-wed, mouthing off against the war

and Frieda, a Richthofen, signalling to subs
they said. But *the* thing now is the cliff walk
from Zennor to Man's Head, (our tipsy adults

drove us sleeping back to town), the spring
of tough grass, dog-faced seals breaking
a restive grid of wind across light across

eddies past Wicca Pool, Mussel Point,
Carn Naun, Pen Enys Point. What beer then?
St Austell Ales, almost certainly.

Kathy Pimlott

A Pint For The Landlord

There should be a pint for the landlord:
no matter that he's been dead three years.
There should be a clean shirt, one that has all
its buttons. There should be a belt on his jeans.

There should be a barber to trim his sideburns
and if there's a doctor, let it be one that gives him
more than six months. There should be a wife
who stays, kids who don't disown him, sheets

on the bed to hide the stains. There should be
a friend with a key, so when it happens,
as it will, as it did, there should be someone
to find him, not leave him five days.

Julie Mellor

Ex-Trawlerman's Beermat Haiku at The Whalebone, Hull

Wine-dark sea? Think beer:
let fish-finings load your pint
with light. Is that clear?

Cliff Forshaw

From the Whalebone

These evenings I step from the Whalebone
At time-on-your-beer for a piss out the back,
And then stand in the mixture of moonlight and sodium,
Waiting and taking it in.
The powdery blue of high summer
Refires the bricks red and black.
There are gaps in the traffic
Where water runs through. And I'm old.
The fifty-year mild-drinking errand
Has carried me this way most nights,
Over ironclad bridges, past tanneries,
Headstones, the grey river glimpsed
As it roars to itself at the bend
To be done with its name in a mile,
And down at the swingbridge the railway sets off
To its vanishing-point, where the houses
And streetlamps run out and the last bus
Turns back. You get all that from here.
It was only the meantime, this amateur city
That never believed where it was.
Behind it the secretive flatlands
Are closed for the night, for the century,
Minding a dialect, a closeness to water
That water is bearing away.
I shall sit on a fly-haunted coach
While it shrugs off the hedgerows and lingers
At shelters where nobody gets on or off,
And then walk the last bit to be sure how it stands,
Grey-green, coming in, the horizon in place
And the atlas beyond it unopened.

Sean O'Brien

Day Trip

In a pub full of all day drinkers, a joke
I couldn't catch
set the table laughing –

one of those days
I couldn't drift or flow

or forget the serious sea
out in the bay where the tide comes in
faster than a man can run.

Julie Lumsden

Pub Crawl Prose

A Few Years In Pubs

There was Grand Central, tucked in by the shoulder of the station, with its rain splattered roof terrace and the trapdoor to the cellar. You had to bend down and heft it up every time a barrel needed changing, step around the void as you pulled pints; it played havoc with your lumbar. Shirted men would dance to Hot Chip, Friday drunk. Monica came to visit you there, once, whilst you were on shift, you were so proud to show her off. Mostly though you'd traipse back down the slope of Trafalgar Street, under the station forecourt, toward No 10 Grand Parade, to see if she'd be waiting in your bed for you or not. Most often not.

There was the Thomas Kemp, up St James' and beyond, a street from the sea; people said back when it had been the Burlington it had hosted the National Front. You'd prance around in a dress and wig and Maia's make-up on New Year's Eve, you'd do laughing gas on the sofas at the back at midnight on a Tuesday with Talin and Desperate Dan the chef—no, you'd abstain, observe, then head to the beach with Dan and Steve before you worked up the courage to try it. You'd take the stretched red balloon to your lips, suck in and hold it, hold it, the wave sound turning into a synth effect, *szzzzzzing, szzzzzzing*, your feet kicking the stones as you slid down the groyne, giggling. Steve's head would appear above you, dazed, saying 'Where's Chris?', before Dan told him to look down.

There was the Duke of Norfolk, the bookshelf-lined box on Western Road, where Scarlet or Tom would DJ, Bill Withers and Herbie Hancock (or is that in your head?), and the lesbians who made up half the bar and kitchen staff or who just liked to party with Ange, the manager, would congregate, dance on the tables, come behind the bar on a Tuesday to put on Florence and the Machine, to roar along like they were at a festival. They'd mostly ignore you. Luke would tell you Sheffield stories, of being a thug ('Really? You? No way ... seriously?'), getting off crack, of his ex having Roots Manuva's baby, of the drunken orgy he'd had in Amsterdam with four Mancunian girls and a Sheffield singer whose identity he would never disclose ('Cocker? Turner? Hawley? C'mon man!'). Mostly you'd close up on drip-drab weeknights, trudge back down Western Road, past the minimarts and kebab shops and late night venues also trying to close, to the bedsit off Russell Square. Maia would be asleep already, a light left on for you, sometimes dinner on a baking tray. She'd be under the covers in a dressing gown, maybe a beanie too if it was really cold, electric heater stood by the bed, costing money. You'd kiss her head, she'd murmur a sleepy hello. You'd read for a bit or watch YouTube videos about the 2012 US election, post Rick Santorum quips on Facebook. Lads would be yammering and drunk-howling as they passed through the square below, out by the squat where a few months later some guy would be murdered. Once you'd got the post-shift hum out of your bones you'd climb in next to her, cuddle for a minute or two, then turn on your side to face the wall, to slip into the spaces of dreams, where walls are moveable, and lovers comingle.

There was Xuma. Up on Seven Dials. Strange little place, a refitted bank, the downstairs office in what used to be the vault. A couple of halfway houses were within spitting distance, and you'd sit at the end of the bar reading Irvine Welsh, John Fante, wondering if you'd have to deal with one of the crackheads. Phil would try his fucking hardest to squeeze a living out of that place, his framed gold record on the floor of the office, leaning against a flakepainted wall, between the piles of paperwork and the spare crisp stock. But he was fighting a losing battle.

You'd keep working there after Maia left, there and Sidewinder, back over in Kemptown. One night you'd even go back to cover a shift at the Thomas Kemp, you and lovely Eve, so the new cadre of Kemp staff could go on a work night out (so unnerving the way the places stay the same whilst all the people change). You'd tell lovely Eve about how you'd met here, worked together, about that New Year's in the dress and make-up. You'd just started seeing her, you say, were barely a couple. You'd got smashed even though you were meant to be running the shift, done coke even though you never do, and after you'd finally got the pub emptied somewhere around six a.m. you'd broken the key off in the front door, stared at it like an idiot. She volunteered to stay and wait for the locksmith, sent you back to her flat to sleep it off, and you'd passed out on her bed, your phone still in your bag in the pub, her keys in your pocket. She'd had to wait until Elaine had finished her shift at Valentino's to get back in, and by then it was almost ten. She'd got an hour's sleep, and the two of you had made your way back to open up for New Year's Day. You spent the next three hours puking into the mop bucket on the floor of the cellar, then sleeping on the sofa in the upstairs flat, then puking into the toilet, whilst she took care of the pub. You eventually made it back downstairs by eight or nine o'clock, to lie on the back sofas sipping lime and soda, wrapped in her fake fur leopard print charity shop coat, mascara crusted around your eyes. And she never once got angry, you tell Eve. She brought you pints of water, checked that you were okay, worked a double shift alone. Did her job, took care of the pub, of you. That was when you knew, you tell Eve.

You walk around the pub that night, as you're closing down. Up and down the staircase, around the back bar, through the little dark garden. All the spaces that are so imprinted in your heart. You inhabit them like a ghost, a figure out of time, like a house that's been sold. Someone else's home.

You don't work in pubs now, you teach at a university. Didn't work in pubs in Thailand or Korea, in those intervening years. But you thought about it, sometimes. Thought about getting a weekend job, some part-time shifts. Joining in with the shots on the back bar, joshing with the drunkards, reprimanding the obnoxious, free-pouring rum and topping up half-pints of cider after you've locked up, smoking with the young staff, feet up on the tables, weed and fags and lemon cleaning gel wafting in the air. Thought about those long, lone, boring weeknights, when you were waiting for closing time, locking up on your own, cashing up on your own, so you could head back down the slopes, seagulls and sirens and night time in the air, back to the small cold room that you shared with the one you loved.

Chris Neilan

Pub Crawl Prose

Last Orders

The past is a pub in Welshpool—let's call it The Talbot—with tudor beams and buttery light from one large window. When you push it, the door is not the heavy oak affair you imagined. Inside, a goal has just been scored on telly and a player in red seems to skid on his knees from the screen out into the room, bringing a surge of noise with him. You step in and, one by one, the men put down their pints in silence to stare you out. The stubble of your newly-shaved head. Your Arctryx climbing jacket, boyfriend jeans. Someone has a conspicuous slurp of John Smiths. You want to take one of the high stools at the bar, but instead you carry your half of Coors to a side room—the one designed for children—and sit alone. You take your notebook out. You start to write.

*

You're eleven and Emma has those gold studs in her ears your dad won't let you get. She leads you down to the cool cellar of her parents' pub. Duckmanton. Ducky Lodge, shy behind overgrown trees on the road to Chesterfield. You're under your childhood street now and it smells of malt. The silver barrels seem to hum, but Emma says its just the fridges. She takes two bottles of cherryade from a box and hands you one and you tip your head back and drink summer and the Spice Girls and white chocolate dip. Outside, there are playing fields and a cricket pitch where you invent murders, find evidence in the bones of small birds. On the last day of the holidays, you play hide and seek. You can hear Emma running away from you. When you open your eyes, you're much taller and the windows of the blue huts by the bowling green are smashed, starred with missing glass.

*

Your step-grandad's family in Birmingham buy you your own pool cue and every Sunday he practices with you in the civil service club. The table has a mauve, fringed lampshade overhead and you prefer looking up into it to potting the colours on the table. Each time your step-grandad goes outside to smoke, you sip from his pint. You feel like a man. After he's dead, you'll go through his things and wonder what happened to the cue.

*

Kayleigh runs the bar at Calow Working Men's Club and can get you cheap Smirnoff Ice. You all go there before town on Saturdays, where you'll stand shivering in the queue for The Beach Bar for hours practicing stories, reciting your fake dates of birth. But the WMC is the best part of the night. Checking your outfits in the mirrorball, listening to songs made before you were born. Decades later when they knock it down, they will leave all the parts on the ground - the crushed jukebox, the broken porcelain toilets, the hand dryer and the notice board. You will walk past every day with your dog and try to spot the shoes you kicked off in there once to walk home barefoot, drunk and cold and barely seventeen.

*

You pull pints for Kenton in The Midland every Sunday. An England flag draped over one window, big Mandy's ferrets scuttling round the bar, making the punters shriek. When she's bored, Mandy steps behind the bar, shoulders you out of the way and tops up her Malibu and coke from the optics. Doubles. Triples. The thrum and rattle of motorbikes outside. A seaside town without the sea. Back at college in Cambridge, you'll talk about the pub and your new friends will laugh and think it's all anecdote. But you're not there yet. You're pouring Stella for a man with three silver hoops in each ear who hunkers down into his biker jacket. He never speaks to you except when his wife calls on his mobile and he passes you the phone. Talk to her. Tell her I'm not a liar. Tell that bitch I'm really here.

*

Smart pubs. Converted pubs. Pubs where they chat to you about Real Ale, places you could take your dad to and say the names of hills neither of you have climbed. A pub called the 'Twa Dogs where they don't let dogs in. A pub on top of the world. Dead pubs. Boarded up pubs. The pub you've been going to with Milner since you were 18. Pubs you cry in. Pubs you don't drive back from. Pubs where the landlord tries to convert you to rum. Pubs with pub quizzes you can never win. Pubs where someone's sister sings Queen on karaoke. The pub where he puts his hand on your knee for the first time and the pub where he puts his hand on your knee seven years later. Pubs you try to remember the names of. Pubs you try to find, again and again in a city you've only been to once because it was good, it was so good and you know it's just round the corner.

*

You and Alan are staying in a Bed and Breakfast in Penrhyndeudraeth with a view of a sloping, grey street and – beyond it – a sliver of the sea. He's just turned 52 and you're about to turn 32 and tomorrow you'll walk up Snowdon from Rhyd Ddu, as you've done nearly every June for the last five years of your friendship. When the B&B owner calls round to check everything is ok, Alan asks if there's a pub in the village he can recommend. He pauses, smiles. There is. And I can't. You imagine the knackered darts board, precarious above your head, the frosty locals and the lukewarm white wine. Part of you will always want to go. Instead, you turn the sofas and decorative table of the B&B into a tap room. You and Alan toast with cups of herbal tea. You talk until midnight, because there's no bell for Time. There's so much to say. You don't know where to start.

Helen Mort

Biographies

Simon Armitage

Simon Armitage's latest collection is *The Unaccompanied*. He is Professor of Poetry at Leeds University and in 2015 was appointed Oxford Professor of Poetry. He doesn't have a local anymore, for reasons documented in this anthology. But Pule Side Working Men's Club was always the boozer of choice, and where he served an occasionally messy apprenticeship to alcohol and sociability. It's still there, still open, clinging on to the side of the moor above Marsden, despite everything that's happened to pubs, clubs, the working classes, and even the moors.

Mike Barlow

Mike Barlow has published three full collections. His first collection *Living on the Difference* (smith|doorstop 2004) won the Poetry Business Book and Pamphlet Competition and was shortlisted for the Jerwood Aldeburgh Prize for best first collection. His third collection is *Charmed Lives* (smith|doorstop 2012). His pamphlet *Amicable Numbers* (Templar 2008) was a Poetry Book Society Pamphlet Choice. He has won a number of competitions, including the 2006 National Poetry Competition. He currently runs Wayleave Press, a small pamphlet publishing venture at www.wayleavepress.co.uk

Tara Bergin

Tara Bergin's second collection, *The Tragic Death of Eleanor Marx*, was published by Carcanet in 2017. Tara is from Dublin and has much experience of pubs. One favourite used to be The Forty Foot in Dun Laoghaire, where she and her fellow workers would go to quench their thirst after a long day selling books.

Rachael Boast

Rachael Boast was born in 1975 and is the author of three collections of poetry from Picador: *Sidereal* (2011), *Pilg* (2013) and *Void Studies* (2016). She was co-editor of *The Echoing Gallery: Bristol Poets* and *Art in the City* (Redcliffe Press). She frequents The Rummer Hotel in Bristol's Old City from where S.T. Coleridge published his radical magazine *The Watchman* in the 1790's. Ahead of his time, Coleridge also delivered some of the first anti-slavery speeches in nearby Corn Street.

Alison Brackenbury

Alison Brackenbury was born in Lincolnshire in 1953. Her ninth collection is *Skies, Carcanet*, 2016, which featured on Radio 4 and in *The Guardian*, and was chosen by *The Observer* as a Poetry Book of the Year. New poems can be read at her website: www.alisonbrackenbury.co.uk. Her favourite pub is The Exmouth Arms, 167 Bath Road, Cheltenham. This hosts poets once a month, ukulele players once a week, and beautiful dogs every day!

Carole Bromley

Carole Bromley has three collections with smith|doorstop, *A Guided Tour of the Ice House*, *The Stonegate Devil* and a collection for children, *Blast Off!*. Her favourite pub is The Lamb and Lion in York.

Colette Bryce

Colette Bryce is a poet from Derry, Northern Ireland. She has published four poetry collections including *The Full Indian Rope Trick* (Picador, 2004) and *Self-Portrait in the Dark* (2008). Her latest, T*he Whole & Rain-domed Universe* (2014), was awarded a special Ewart-Biggs Award in memory of Seamus Heaney in 2015. She currently lives in the north of England where she works as a freelance writer and editor. She received the Cholmondeley Award for poetry in 2010. Her favourite pub is Sandinos in Derry: great music, politics, and a lovely pint of Guinness.

Alan Buckley

Alan Buckley was brought up on Merseyside. His debut pamphlet *Shiver* was a Poetry Book Society Choice; his second pamphlet *The Long Haul* was published by Happen*Stance* in 2016. He now lives in Oxford, where he works as a trauma-focused psychotherapist for a refugee charity. His favourite pub is The Goat Hotel in Llanfair Caereinion, Powys; he goes there once a month for dinner with friends, before getting soundly beaten by the local pool sharks.

James Caruth

James Caruth was born in Belfast but now lives in Sheffield. His first collection *A Stones Throw* (Staple) was published 2007 followed by a long poem sequence *Dark Peak* (Longbarrow, 2007). He has had two pamphlets published by smith|doorstop, *Marking the Lambs* (2012) and *The Death of Narrative*, which was winner of The Poetry Business Competition 2014. He currently has two favourite pubs – McDaids, Henry Street, Dublin and The Grapes, Sheffield.

Brendan Cleary

Brendan Cleary is originally from Co. Antrim. He has published many full-length collections & pamphlets. He lives in Brighton & depending on his mood he drinks in either The Great Eastern or The Gladstone

Oliver Comins

Oliver Comins' third short collection *Battling Against the Odds* (2017) includes 18 golf hole poems and follows *Yes to Everything* (2014) and *Staying in Touch* (2015), all published by Templar. Earlier poems were collected in *Playing out time in an awkward light* (Mandeville 1993) and *Anvil New Poets Two* (1995). His favourite pub is the Virgins & Castle in Kenilworth.

Angela Croft

Angela Croft spent much of her childhood in Cornwall and finds relaxing in the bar of the Falmouth Hotel with its panoramic view of the sea is hard to beat. She took to writing poetry following a career in journalism and her pamphlet *Dancing with Chagall*, was published in Caboodle by ProleBooks. Her poems also appear on a number of websites including the Poetry Kit and she has been widely published in newspapers and magazines from The North to The South, all kept safe in a laundry bag under her table.

Angelina D'Roza

Angelina D'Roza's collection, *Envies the Birds*, was published by Longbarrow Press (2016). Her favourite pub is The Grapes in Sheffield.

Michael di Placido

Michael Di Placido was born in Scarborough and has published collections with both smith|doorstop and Valley Press. The Vic, formerly the Victoria Hotel and now known as The Old Vic, was a favourite watering hole in the halcyon years of his early twenties. The iconic building, opposite Scarborough Railway Station, was the childhood home of the actor Charles Laughton who achieved global fame as a Hollywood movie star. Indeed, it was in the then Charles Laughton Bar where those impromptu Sinatra renditions were delivered – whether requested or not!
Great, turbulent days. Enough, it would seem, to have inspired a poem.

Jonathan Davidson

Jonathan Davidson is a poet and dramatist. He lives in the Midlands. He drinks in many pubs, most recently in The Lord Clifton on Great Hampton Street in Birmingham. The beer was reasonably priced and of a certain quality. There were salt and vinegar crisps, the one, true flavour. The clientele was mixed and friendly. Had he wished he could have played table tennis in the pub garden, which is always nice.

Steve Dearden

Steve Dearden's collection of short stories *Single Skin* is published by smith|doorstop. As Writer in Residence for the 2013/14 Wakefield Literature Festivals he wrote the online novella www.wakelost.com. He was also Writer in Residence at Bluewater Shopping Centre for ARCHItexts and has been published in anthologies from Route and Comma Press as well as magazines in the UK, Finland and Australia. He runs the Writing Squad, developing the next generation of writers in the north. After living in Durham and Yorkshire he has returned to Manchester. www.stevedearden.com

Maura Dooley

Maura Dooley's latest publications are *The Silvering* and *A Quire of Paper*. She is working, with Elhum Shakerifar, on a collection of poems by the exiled Iranian poet Azita Ghahreman. She lives in London and teaches at Goldsmiths College. Her favourite pubs used to be The Ferryboat Inn at Wheldrake (currently resting) and The Blue Bell, Fossgate, York. She lives near the magnificent Bedford, Balham, a South London institution.

Ian Duhig

Ian Duhig has written seven books of poetry, most recently *The Blind Roadmaker* (Picador 2016), shortlisted for the Roehampton, Forward Best Collection and TS Eliot Prizes. He lives in Leeds where his true favourite pub, The Roscoe, was demolished to make way for the Sheepscar Interchange; his new favourite is the nearest to his house, the Nag's Head, where poet John Riley and Surrealist artist Tony Earnshaw were regulars. He sits there silently with their ghosts sometimes, all three waiting for one of the others to buy a round. A former homelessness worker, Duhig is currently developing a piece for Refugee Tales.

Steven Earnshaw

Steven Earnshaw's *The Pub in Literature: England's Altered State* was published in 2000, tracing the role of the pub in drama, poetry and the novel from Chaucer through to the end of the twentieth century. *Memory Clinic*, a collection of short stories, was published in 2016, and he is currently completing work on The Existential Drinker, which looks at fictional protagonists who commit their lives to drinking. Favourite Sheffield pubs are The Rutland in town and The White Lion at Heeley.

Steve Ely

Steve Ely has published four collections of poetry, most recently *Werewolf* (Calder Valley Poetry) and *Incendium Amoris* (Smokestack Books). His biographical work, *Ted Hughes's South Yorkshire: Made in Mexborough*, is published by Palgrave Macmillan. He lectures in Creative Writing at the University of Huddersfield where he is Director of the Ted Hughes Network. His favourite pub is the Tap & Barrel in Ponty.

Suzannah Evans

Suzannah Evans lives in Sheffield and has published a pamphlet of poems, *Confusion Species*, a winner in the 2012 Poetry Business Competition. Her pub poems are nostalgic for pubs with jukeboxes: James's in Bewdley, Worcestershire in the late 90s and the Castle Hotel, Aberystwyth between 2001-2005. Her current favourite pub is the Broadfield Ale House in Sheffield.

John Fennelly

Poet. Barman in Lewisham and Kilkenny. House Poet at MMU for Carol Ann Duffy and Friends, Royal Exchange, Manchester. Pubs: Royal Inn (Hackney), The Fellowship (Bellingham), The French (Soho), The Vale Cottage (Gorton, Manchester), The Golden Tiger (Prague), The Meat Market and Singer Bar (Czeske Budijoveice) and all the pubs in Brno, especially Dessert and The Last Hunt. That's not even scratched the surface of the Pub Bio, how many words left for the Poe ...

John Foggin

John Foggin lives in West Yorkshire, writes a poetry blog: the great fogginzo's cobweb, and jointly organises the Puzzle Poets Live in Sowerby Bridge. A prize winner in the 2016 Poetry Business Book and Pamplet Competition, his first full collection, *Much Possessed* is published by smith|doorstop (November 2016). There have been too many pubs in his life; the best was probably The Shakespeare Tavern (the back room) in Durham.

Cliff Forshaw

Cliff Forshaw is a poet and painter. He has been writer-in-residence in California, France, Romania and Tasmania, twice a Hawthornden Writing Fellow, and guest poet at the Festival Internacional de Poesía de Granada in Nicaragua 2016. Collections include *Vandemonian* (Arc, 2013) and Pilgrim Tongues (Wrecking Ball Press, 2015). A satirical sequence illustrated by Cliff's paintings and drawings, Satyr, is due from *Shoestring* in 2017. His favourite pub is an old Beverley coaching inn with open fires, wonky tables and very cheap Sam Smith's; though officially called The White Horse, everyone knows it as Nellie's.

Annie Freud
Annie Freud is a poet and artist. She has three collection with Picador, *The Best Man That Ever Was*, *The Mirabelles* and *The Remains*.
Her favourite pub is The Fox and Hounds in Cattistock.

Moira Garland
Some of Moira Garland's best times were in the 1960s at The Lowther, York, refining her drinking, darts and snooker skills. She later discovered a taste for real ale in Huddersfield and Leeds. Her interests include melodeon playing for a women's Morris side, and sewing clothes that don't always fit. Her short fiction is in print and online; her poetry has been published and won prizes. She is here: @moiragauthor and here: www.wordswords-moirag.blogspot.co.uk

Sally Goldsmith
Sally Goldsmith lives on the edge of Sheffield near the Peak District. Her favourite pub is the Red Lion at Litton, Derbyshire because of her 1950s caravan, which sits conveniently and disreputably behind it. Sally is a script and songwriter as well as a poet, a historian, utopian, environmentalist, a very amateur naturalist and a bad learner of Dutch. Her first pamphlet *Singer* was a winner in the Poetry Business Pamphlet Competition, judged by Michael Longley and her full-length collection, *Are We There Yet?* was published by smith|doorstop in 2013.

Mark Hailwood
Mark Hailwood is a Lecturer in the History of England in the period 1400 to 1700, at the University of Bristol. He spent much of his youth and young manhood in and around the pubs of the North Somerset town of Portishead, which inspired his interest in the institution's history. Mark is author of *Alehouses and Good Fellowship in Early Modern England*, and a co-ordinator of the Drinking Studies Network, a collective of academics from any and all disciplines who share a serious interest in the role alcohol plays in society, past and present.

Ramona Herdman
Ramona Herdman's pamphlet is published by Happen*Stance*. Her first collection *Come what you wished for* was published by Egg Box in 2003.

She tweets occasionally @ramonaherdman. Her old favourite pub has lost its scruffy sofas and is now all uplighters and fancy spirits, so shall remain nameless.

A B Jackson

A B Jackson was born in Glasgow in 1965 and grew up in the village of Bramhall, Cheshire. After moving to Cupar in Fife he studied English Literature at the University of Edinburgh and went on to work as a library systems manager for NHS Scotland. His first book, *Fire Stations* (Anvil), won the Forward Prize for Best First Collection in 2003, and a pamphlet, *Apocrypha* (Donut Press), was published in 2011. His second full-length collection, *The Wilderness Party* (Bloodaxe Books, 2015), is a Poetry Book Society Recommendation. In 2010 he won first prize in the Edwin Morgan International Poetry Competition. He has a PhD in Creative Writing from Sheffield Hallam University and currently works at Cambridge University Library.

Wendy Klein

Wendy Klein was born in New York, brought up in California and didn't write poetry or visit pubs until after she came to England in 1971. She has three collections from UK publishers Cinnamon Press and Oversteps Books. Her favourite pub after much diligent research is still The New Inn at Kidmore End, Oxon, though The Witch in Lindfield, mid-Sussex is gaining ground fast.

Martin Kratz

Martin Kratz lives in Manchester. He imagines his Skeleton Man poems as a kind of cartoon strip without pictures. The most curious drinking establishment he has been to was the Downtown Hotel in Dawson City, Canada. The hotel bar is the home of the infamous Sourtoe Cocktail, whose main ingredient is a severed human toe ...

Zaffar Kunial

Zaffar Kunial was born in Birmingham and lives in Hebden Bridge. His poetry pamphlet was published by Faber & Faber in 2014 as part of the Faber New Poets series.

Andrew Lambeth

Andrew Lambeth's editioned hand-bound work is in the private collections of Jacob Polley, Carol Mavor, Jungleyes Cism Love and others. The Dirty Dicks on Blackfriars Lane, at the foot of Ludgate Hill, had the deepest cellars in all of London when he was a boy. His dog was allowed in, he wasn't. Dirty Dicks wasn't the name of the pub – people just called it that. And anyway, it's gone.

Grevel Lindop

Grevel Lindop lives in Manchester, where he formerly taught at the University and is now a freelance writer. His work includes biographies of Thomas De Quincey and Charles Williams, *Travels on the Dance Floor* (about salsa in Latin America), *A Literary Guide to the Lake District*, and seven collections of poems from Carcanet. His website is www.grevel.co.uk. His favourite Manchester pub used to be Tommy Duck's, where the bar ceiling was covered in ladies' knickers and the back wall was covered in men's snipped-off ties; but it was demolished to make way for a car park; so he now has resort to the Briton's Protection or the Peveril of the Peak.

Jane Lovell

Jane Lovell has had work published in a variety of anthologies and journals including *Agenda, Earthlines, Poetry Wales, the North, Dark Mountain* and *Zoomorphic*. She won the Flambard Prize in 2015 and was recently shortlisted for the Basil Bunting Prize. Jane is currently working on her first collection for Agenda Editions. Her favourite pub is The Pepperbox Inn, Harrietsham, Kent.

Julie Lumsden

Julie Lumsden is not a Poet of Place. Born into an army family, she grew up in Kent, Northampton, Singapore, Shrewsbury, Germany and Nottingham. She then studied at Manchester School of Theatre. She now lives in Chesterfield. Poems have most recently appeared in *Stand, the North, The Frogmore Papers* and Hallam University anthology, *Millstone Grit*. A pamphlet, *True Crime*, was published by Shoestring. Her favourite pub is the Old Queens Head, which is the oldest occupied domestic building in Sheffield, thought to date from 1475. It stands so bravely alone and different, near to the Sheffield Interchange.

Stuart Maconie

Stuart Maconie is a TV and radio presenter, journalist, columnist and best-selling author. His book *Adventures on the High Teas* was the top selling travel book of 2009 and *Pies and Prejudice* was one of 2008's top selling paperbacks. His work has been compared with Bill Bryson, Alan Bennett and John Peel and he has been described by *The Times* as a 'National Treasure'. He co-hosts the Radcliffe and Maconie Show on BBC Radio 6Music, as well as The Freak Zone and The Freakier Zone on 6Music. His favourite pub is the Boot & Shoe, Greystoke, Lake District and The Plough, Harborne, Birmingham.

Antony Mair

Antony Mair lives in Hastings. He has had poems accepted for publication in numerous magazines and in several anthologies. He won first prize in the Rottingdean Writers National Poetry Competition 2016 and was shortlisted in the Live Canon Poetry Competition 2016. From the desk in his study he looks out to sea on one side and down a small hill on the other, at the bottom of which is The Crown, recently refurbished into an award-winning hostelry. There are no mermaids, but in spite of this deficiency it has to rank as his favourite pub.

Roy Marshall

Roy Marshall's poetry collections *The Sun Bathers* and *The Great Animator* are published by Nottingham's Shoestring Press. He has fond memories of the pubs of St. Albans in the nineteen-eighties. There were fifty-two pubs in the town at the time and one of the best, the now extinct Midland Railway, had a pool table and a very loud juke box that played singles by Free, Thin Lizzie and Led Zeppelin in the age of Bucks Fizz.

Ellen McAteer

Ellen McAteer is a librarian, poet, songwriter, and visiting lecturer with the Glasgow School of Art. Her favourite pubs are the Locks Inn at Geldeston and the State Bar in Glasgow.

Michael McCarthy

Michael McCarthy was born in West Cork and lives in North Yorkshire. Winner of the Patrick Kavanagh Award, his most recent collection *The Healing Station* was described by Anne Enright as 'life at its most challenging made beautiful on the page,' and chosen by Hilary Mantel in *The Guardian* Best Books 2015. He's not a drinker, but as a subsistence cook has lunch in a pub most days – favourites at the moment are The Oddfellows in Sherburn in Elmet and the Cross Keys at Hillam.

John McCullough

John McCullough's first collection of poems *The Frost Fairs* won the Polari First Book Prize in 2012. His new collection *Spacecraft* was named one of T*he Guardian*'s Best Books for Summer 2016. He worked as a barman for two years at The Bulldog in Brighton, and now lives in Hove. He teaches creative writing at New Writing South and the Open University.

Andrew McMillan

Andrew McMillan's debut collection *physical* was the first ever poetry collection to win *The Guardian* First Book Award; it also won a Somerset Maugham Award, an Eric Gregory Award and the Fenton Aldeburgh First Collection Prize. It was shortlisted for The Dylan Thomas Prize and the Costa Poetry Award, amongst others. He lectures in Creative Writing at Manchester Metropolitan University. The Thompson Arms, or Thompsons as it's colloquially known, is on the edge of Manchester's gay village and the epicentre of a lot of my formative experiences.

Julie Mellor

Julie Mellor lives near Sheffield and holds a PhD from Sheffield Hallam University. Her first pamphlet, *Breathing Through Our Bones*, was published in 2012 and her second pamphlet, *Out of the Weather*, was published in 2017 by smith|doorstop. She blogs at http://juliemellorpoetsite.wordpress.com Her favourite pub is tied between The Huntsman, Thurlstone, and The Nook, Holmfirth.

Kim Moore

Kim Moore was a winner in the 2011 Poetry Business Book and Pamphlet Competition with her pamphlet *If We Could Speak Like Wolves*. The pamphlet was shortlisted for the Michael Marks Award and named in the Independent as a Book of the Year. Her full length collection *The Art of Falling* was published by Seren in 2015. She is currently a PhD candidate at Manchester Metropolitan University. Her favourite pub is The Palace in Leeds, where she was a music student, despite not having been in for 14 years. When she thinks of it now, she still remembers the feeling of hovering between possibilities, excitement and boredom mixed together, the feeling of being on the edge of a beginning or an ending.

Helen Mort

Helen Mort is a poet from Sheffield. Her collection *Division Street* was published in 2013 and shortlisted for the T.S. Eliot Prize and the Costa Prize. In 2014, she won the Fenton Aldeburgh Prize for best first collection. She has also published several pamphlets including *A Pint For the Ghost*, a Poetry Book Society Choice. In 2014, Helen was selected for the Poetry Book Society's Next Generation promotion, recognising the 20 most exciting new poets from the UK and Ireland.

Graham Mort

Graham Mort's latest collection of poetry, *Black Shiver Moss*, was published by Seren in 2017. His favourite pub is the fabulous White Bear in Oldham. It's staffed by the flame-haired ghosts of barmen and maids. Along the bar, a quartet of cocked beer engines, a line of half-full pints ringed by foam. The blues band are stumbling through their final number. Last orders. A benediction of slurred curses. Blurred laughter. A brass foot-rail glittering. Etched glass and mahogany spinning us to the street. Surprising rain. A painted bear dancing, a lit bus passing: the long walk home to dawn.

Chris Neilan

Chris Neilan is an author, screenwriter and filmmaker, and associate lecturer in creative writing at Manchester Metropolitan University. He has swilled soju and makeolli in Chungcheong province, and chugged pinkish cocktails by the Andaman ocean, but his favourite pub remains the Thomas Kemp in Brighton, circa 2009-2010: cider on a Sunday after a packed shift, roast pork steaming up the windows and Tuaca for a pound, with the beach gulls cawing in the beer garden.

Greta Nintzel

Greta Nintzel's sense of home is a bit wobbly. She was born in Manhasset, NY (on Long Island) and has lived in New England, Florida, North Carolina and Seattle, WA. These kinds of shifts from place to place across regions with varied personalities make a good pub a welcome spot to land and reorient. Her favourite is Sun Liquor in Seattle, WA. Her poems have appeared in *The North*, *Magma* and a number of US literary journals.

Sean O'Brien

Sean O'Brien's ninth collection of poems, *Europa*, is due from Picador in Spring 2018. He is Professor of Creative Writing at Newcastle University. His favourite pub at the moment is The Hotspur at Haymarket in Newcastle. It's a friendly city centre pub with a mixed clientele. My God, that sounds boring. And you can hear yourself think.

Mark Pajak

Mark Pajak was born in Merseyside. His poetry has been highly commended in the National Poetry Competition and won a Northern Writers' Award from New Writing North. His poem 'Spitting Distance' won first place in the 2016 Bridport Prize and his debut pamphlet, of the same name, is one of the 2016 Laureate's Choice series published by smith|doorstop. The Fosters Arms, Bridgnorth, was the first pub to serve Mark alcohol (he was 13).

Kathy Pimlott

Kathy Pimlott's pamphlet *Goose Fair Night* was published in 2016. She lives in Seven Dials, London, home of the ballad and the broadsheet. Her favourite pub, before it was turned into a winebar, was The Peacock in Maiden Lane. Quiet, with plenty of seats, it was patronised almost entirely by the backstage staff and sceneshifters from the nearby theatres – often during the shows.

Clare Pollard

Clare Pollard's latest collection is *Incarnation* (Bloodaxe, 2017). Her favourite pub is The Belle Vue in Ramsgate for the view, although she'd like it even better if it served Aspall Cider.

D A Prince

D A Prince lives in Leicestershire and London. Her second collection (*Common Ground,* HappenStance Press) won the East Midlands Book Award 2015. Out of all the Suffolk pubs her favourite is The Eel's Foot, Eastbridge, far from main roads and their traffic, and the habitat of bird-watchers, walkers, and house sparrows.

Antony Rowland

Antony Rowland has published two poetry collections: *The Land of Green Ginger* (Salt, 2008) and *I Am a Magenta Stick* (Salt, 2012). He was awarded the Manchester Poetry Prize in 2012 for work now published in a collection by Arc in 2017. His poems have been anthologised in *Identity Parade: New British and Irish Poets* (Bloodaxe, 2010), and *New Poetries III* (Carcanet, 2003). He received an Eric Gregory Award from the Society of Authors in 2000, and recorded for the national Poetry Archive in 2009. His favourite pub is The Fighting Cock in Bradford.

Jon Sayers

Jon Sayers grew up in Elstree, Hertfordshire. His poems and translations have been published in leading UK magazines. His radio play *A World Full of Weeping*, a supernatural thriller featuring the poetry of Yeats, was twice broadcast on Radio 4. Jon works as a verbal identity specialist and teacher and is currently training with the National Association for Poetry Therapy in the USA. His favourite local is the Rose & Crown in Waterloo. The pub in his poem is The Waggon & Horses, Elstree.

Tom Sastry

Following a period of extensive research, Tom Sastry chose to live a few doors down from The Hillgrove in Bristol, where he wrote the first draft of this poem.

Ann Sansom

Ann Sansom's books include *Romance* and *In Praise of Men & Other People* (Bloodaxe). She is co-director of The Poetry Business. When she worked at the Women's Centre, the pub across the road was The Saracen's Head – unless there was a phone call, in which case it was 'I'll just check. I think she's in The Office', and someone would pelt across and hook you off the pool table, where you were just restoring yourself after a difficult morning/night. It was a quiet pub with stained glass, plush seats, big ashtrays and you could order a pint without any trouble. And sit and drink it in peace (At the Admiral you had to order two halves if you were a lady.). She once found a note on her desk, *gone over to the Sarash saras fuckit we're at the Eagle.* Not likely – the Eagle landlady had barred everybody after the only poetry reading they ever had, for dancing like lesbians. The police rolled up. The landlord said he'd have booked us, not barred us.

Peter Sansom

Peter Sansom's books include *Selected Poems* (Carcanet) and *Writing Poems* (Bloodaxe). He is co-director of The Poetry Business. He likes the Cheshire Cheese between Hope and Edale in the Peak District. It's a fourteenth century inn with a proper open fire, not-dear pub meals and a starry walk back to wherever you've been able to park your car along the windy lane. It also has a great pub quiz that four of the Poetry Business team once actually won – Suzannah getting the ornithology and animals and Ellen, among other things, crucially identifying a dry-clean only label. Peter knew one about Kylie Minogue and Ann got all the rest.

Catherine Smith

Catherine Smith was born in Windsor and did most of her underage drinking in The Two Brewers pub, adjacent to the town's castle. She has published three full collections and two pamphlets. Twice forwarded for the Forward Prize, and selected as a 'Next Generation' poet in 2004, she also writes fiction and drama, and teaches creative writing. Her favourite pub is The Lewes Arms in Lewes, East Sussex.

Martin Stannard

Martin Stannard's most recent collection is *Poems for the Young at Heart* (Leafe Press, 2016). He has been living and teaching in China since 2005, except for the academic year 2007/8 when he was the Royal Literary Fund's Writing Fellow at Nottingham Trent University. He is currently Poetry Editor for *Decals of Desire*, an online magazine of art and poetry (decalsofdesire. blogspot.com). As for a favourite pub, there's always something of a soft spot for The Peacock on the Mansfield Road in Nottingham – some good memories of some good people

Paul Stephenson

Paul Stephenson has published two pamphlets. His first *Those People* (2015), published by smith|doorstop, a winner in The Poetry Business competition judged by Billy Collins. His second, *The Days that Followed Paris* (2016), was published by Happen*Stance*. He grew up in the village of Great Wilbraham, outside Cambridge. His home, a cottage built in 1741, was once a pub, probably called The Grapes. There were once five pubs in the village but now only one, The Carpenter's Arms, where his mother worked weekday lunchtimes while he was at school. In the neighbouring village of Little Wilbraham is The Hole in the Wall, a fine food pub popular with Newmarket's horse racing community. He used to be a regular of The Free Press just opposite his college room in central Cambridge, which back then banned mobile phones.

Greta Stoddart

Greta Stoddart was born in Oxfordshire in 1966. Her first collection *At Home in the Dark* (Anvil) was shortlisted for the Forward Prize for Best First Collection and won the Geoffrey Faber Memorial Prize in 2002. Her second book, *Salvation Jane* (Anvil), was shortlisted for the Costa Book Award 2008. She was also shortlisted for the Forward Prize for Best Individual Poem in 2012. Her third book, *Alive Alive O* (Bloodaxe, 2015), was shortlisted for the Roehampton Poetry Prize 2016. Her latest work, a radio poem called 'Who's there?' was broadcast on BBC Radio 4 in 2017 and was BBC Pick of the Week. She lives in Devon and teaches for the Poetry School and the Arvon Foundation. Her favourite pub is The Fountainhead in Branscombe, Devon. It's a 14th century old forge with an open fire in the middle of the room, and no music or TV – just photos of the 2007 Napoli shipwreck on the walls to remind you the 'wreckers' history of the area continues ...

Alicia Stubbersfield

Alicia Stubbersfield is Writer-in-Residence for Gloucester Academy as part of the Cheltenham Festivals/First Story project. She is an Arvon tutor, particularly involved with their 'Teachers as Writers' courses. Her most recent poetry collection is *The Yellow Table* (Pindrop Press 2013). Alicia is from the North-West but is now living in Cheltenham with a cat and a lodger. Her favourite pub, although she hasn't been there for some time, is the, more-or-less unchanged, Arden Arms in Stockport.

Sarah Stutt

Sarah Stutt lives in Beverley, East Yorkshire. Her first pamphlet *Winter Born* was published by Poetry Salzburg in 2016. Her favourite pub has always been Nellies (aka The White Horse Inn) in Beverley.

Matthew Sweeney

Matthew Sweeney's most recent collection, *Inquisition Lane*, came out from Bloodaxe in 2015. His previous collection, *Horse Music* (Bloodaxe, 2013) won the inaugural Piggott Poetry Prize. A new book, *My Life as a Painter*, will appear from Bloodaxe in 2018, and a book of prose poems, *King of a Rainy Country*, from Arc.

His favourite pub remains The Lamb, at the far end of Lamb's Conduit Street from where he used to live in Holborn, but the budgie poem happened at another pub halfway down Lamb's Conduit Street which used to be called The Sun (now renamed), while its companion, slightly smaller pub, The Moon, was a street or so away.

Marjorie Sweetko

Majorie Sweetko was born in Canada and lived for many years in London and Sussex, before teaching in Rabat, Bangkok and Bologna and winding up, strangely enough, in Marseille. Her poetry appears regularly in British poetry journals. Her favourite pub is The Cricketers in Broadwater, Worthing.

David Tait

David Tait's first collection *Self-Portrait with The Happiness* was shortlisted for the Fenton Aldeburgh First Collection Prize and received an Eric Gregory Award. His latest pamphlet, *Three Dragon Day*, was a winner in The Poetry Business Pamphlet Competition and was shortlisted for The Michael Marks Award. He lives in Nanjing, China. His favourite pub is a The Fox and Goose in Hebden Bridge, a pub of dogs, chatty old men, incomplete chess sets and a fine array of world beers.

Maria Taylor

Maria Taylor is a poet and reviewer living in Leicestershire. Her first collection *Melanchrini* (Nine Arches Press) was shortlisted for the Michael Murphy Memorial Prize. Her most recent pamphlet, *Instructions for Making Me*, was published in 2016 by Happen*Stance* Press. She blogs at: miskinataylor.blogspot.co.uk. Maria Taylor drinks vodka and diet coke (single, ice and a slice please) at The Moon and Bell in Loughborough.

Pam Thompson

Pam Thompson is a poet and university lecturer based in Leicester. Pam was a winner of The Poetry Business competition in 2005 with her pamphlet, *Show Date and Time*, (Smith-Doorstop, 2006). Other publications include *Spin* (Waldean Press, 1998) and *The Japan Quiz'* (Redbeck Press, 2009). Pam is one of the organisers of Word!, a spoken-word, open-mic night at The Y Theatre in Leicester. Pam has a PhD in Creative Writing from De Montfort University.

Pam's blog is Heckle http://www. pamthompsonpoetry.wordpress.com. Her favourite pub is The Classroom as you get to sit at school desks and drink wine.

John Wedgwood Clarke

John Wedgwood Clarke currently lectures in English Literature and Creative Writing at the University of Hull. His first collection, *Ghost Pot*, was published by Valley Press in 2013. His new collection is *Landfill*, also from Valley Press, published in 2017. He regularly works with scientists and other artists on collaborative public-art projects. His favourite pub is the Tinners Arms at Zennor after walking the coast path from his hometown St Ives -- either in the snug after breathtaking rain, or the garden as a cloud enters from off the Atlantic.

Linda Lee Welch

Linda Lee Welch was born and raised in the USA. She come to England as a student, did her course, joined a band and never went back. She has had two novels published by Virago Press and many poems, songs and stories published in a variety of places. She has been a naturalized Yorkshirewoman for many years, calling Sheffield her home.

Tim Wells

Tim Wells is made of reggae, lager top, pie and mash, and Leyton Orient FC. He drinks amply at the Mascara Bar, usually on grumpy corner.

Ben Wilkinson

Ben Wilkinson is a poet, critic and lecturer at the University of Bolton. His debut collection of poems, *Way More Than Luck*, is due from Seren in 2018. When not training for the marathon, he can often be found drinking in pubs across Sheffield's hills. After Monday night mileage with running pals, cask ales in the Robin Hood at Millhouses are a must.

Anthony Wilson

Anthony Wilson is a poet, writing tutor, blogger and Senior Lecturer at the University of Exeter. His most recent books are *Lifesaving Poems* (Bloodaxe, 2015) and *Riddance* (Worple Press, 2012). His favourite pub is The Wykham Arms in Sibford Gower, after a long walk with the dogs and family. They do not show football.

Luke Wright

Luke Wright tours his poetry all over the world. He is the author of nine solo poetry shows, two collections of poems and two verse plays. The first of these, *What I Learned From Johnny Bevan*, won a prestigious Fringe First Award in 2015. Luke is a regular on BBC radio and television and curates the spoken word line-ups at Port Eliot, Festival No.6, and Edinburgh International Book Festival.

Cliff Yates

Cliff Yates was born in Birmingham. Collections include *Henry's Clock* (smith|doorstop, 1999), winner of the Aldeburgh First Collection Prize and the Poetry Business Book & Pamphlet Competition, *Frank Freeman's Dancing School* (Salt, 2009; Knives Forks and Spoons, 2015) and *Jam* (smith/doorstop, 2016). His favourite pub is The Woolpack in Slad.

Miranda Yates

Miranda Yates lives in Manchester. She was one of the Aldeburgh Eight poets in 2015 and has published her poetry in numerous magazines including *Poetry Review*, the *Rialto*, *Magma* and *the North*. Her favourite country pub is the Cod and Lobster in Staithes. Her favourite city pub is Biddle Bros in Lower Clapton.

Acknowledgments

Many of these poems have been previously published in individual collections, anthologies and anthologies. They are reprinted with kind permission of the below:

Simon Armitage
'The Slaughtered Lamb' was published in *Tyrannosaurus Rex Versus the Corduroy Kid* (Faber & Faber, 2006)

Mike Barlow
'Parish' was previously published in *The North*

Tara Bergin
'The Passion Flower' was published in *This is Yarrow* (Carcanet Press, 2013)

Rachael Boast
'Downtime' was published in *Sidereal* (Picador, 2001)

Carole Bromley
'All the Pubs Where We Used to Meet Are Sinking' was published in *Watermarks: Poems for Hebden Bridge*

Brendan Cleary
'Gift', 'Marina' and 'Sunday Afternoon' were published in *Some Turbulent Weather* (Tall Lighthouse, 2008). 'It's Our Dance' appeared in *Face* (Pighog Press, 2013)

Oliver Comins
'Bar Staff' was previously published in *Giant Steps* (1987) and *Anvil New Poets Two* (1995)

Angela Croft
'Beached' was first published in South, and subsequently in *Peloton* (Templar, 2013) and *Caboodle* (Prole Books)

Jonathan Davidson
'Poem' was published in *Early Train* (smith|doorstop, 2011)

Mike Di Placido
'The Vic' was published in *A Sixty-Watt Las Vegas* (Valley Press, 2013)

Ian Duhig
'Roisin Ban' was previously published in *Jericho Shanty* (Picador, 2009)

Cliff Forshaw
'Ex-Trawlerman's Beermat Haiku at The Whalebone, Hull' appeared as part of a haiku sequence in *Pilgrim Tongues* (Wrecking Ball Press, 2015)

Mark Hailwood
Extract taken from *Alehouses and Good Fellowship in Early Modern England* (Boydell and Brewer, 2014)

Ramona Herdman
An earlier version of 'Ship in a Bottle' was published *the Mill Anthology* (Templar, 2015)

A B Jackson
'Lauder's Bar' and 'Saturday Night' were published in *Fire Stations* (Anvil, 2003)

Grevel Lindop
'Ye Olde Trip to Jerusalem' was published in *The North* issue 57
'The Barrel-Dance' was published in *Selected Poems* (Carcanet Press, 2000)

Stuart Maconie
Extract taken from *The Pie at Night: In Search of the North at Play* (Ebury Books, 2015)

Michael McCarthy
'Scarf' was published in *At the Races* (smith|doorstop, 2009)

John McCullough
'Masterclass' first appeared in *The Frost Fairs* (Salt, 2011)

Greta Nintzel
'Gin Fizz' was first published in *Magma* issue 52

Sean O'Brien
'From the Whalebone' was first published in *The North* in 1991 and since in *Collected Poems* (Picador, 2000)

Mark Pajak
'After Closing Time' is published in the pamphlet *Spitting Distance* (smith|doorstop, 2016)

Clare Pollard
'The Nursery Rhymes' and 'The Lambeth Crawl' were commissioned for *Look Up London* (Freight Books, 2014)

Catherine Smith
'Snakebite' and 'Set of Optics' were both published in *Lip* (smith|doorstop, 2008)

Paul Stephenson
'The Estimate' was published in *Selfie with Waterlillies* (Paper Swans Press, 2017)

Greta Stoddart
'The Night We Stole a Full-Length Mirror' was first published in *The North* in 2000 and since in *At Home in the Dark* (Anvil, 2001)

Matthew Sweeney
'Mackie' and 'The Man with a Budgie on his Back' were published in *Blue Shoes* (Secker & Warburg, 1989)

Linda Lee Welch
'Water and Weight' was previously published in *The North*

Anthony Wilson
'Two Halves' was published in *Nowhere Better Than This* (Worple, 2002)

Luke Wright
'Houses That Used to be Boozers' was published in *What I Learned from Johnny Bevan* (Penned in the Margins, 2015)

Cliff Yates
'On the Third Day' was published in *Frank Freeman's Dancing School* (Salt, 2009 & Knives, Forks and Spoons, 2015)

Index of poems & first lines